THE TWELFTH HOUSE

THE TWELFTH HOUSE

The Hidden Power in the Horoscope

Karen Hamaker-Zondag

SAMUEL WEISER, INC.

York Beach, Maine

First published in 1992 by
Samuel Weiser, Inc.
Box 612
York Beach, Maine 03910-0612

02 01 00 99 98 97 96 95
11 10 9 8 7 6 5 4 3 2

Translated by Transcript, Ltd.

Library of Congress Cataloging-in-Publication Data
Hamaker-Zondag, Karen.
    [Twaalfde huis. English]
  The twelfth house / Karen Hamaker-Zondag.
    p. cm.
  Translation of : Het twaalfde huis.
  Includes bibliographical references.
    1. Houses (Astrology)   I. Title.   II. Title: 12th house.
BF1716.H3613   1991
133.5'3—dc20   91-28354
ISBN 0-87728-727-9   CIP
BJ

Cover painting copyright ©1992 Peggy Carol. Reproduced by permission.

Typeset in 10 point Garamond

Printed in the United States of America

The paper used in this publication meets the minimum requirements of the American National Standard for Permanence of Paper for Printed Library Materials Z39.48-1984.

Contents

Foreword

This book sees the fulfillment of my long-cherished wish to write about the house that has been the subject of so much fear and misunderstanding, and yet is richer and fuller than many other houses in the chart—the 12th. Of course, I myself have suffered experiences that we assign to the negative influences of the 12th house, but I would not have missed them for the world. The results turned out to be much more beneficial than I could possibly have imagined.

It was a series of very impressive dreams back in the 70's that revealed the connection between Jung's psychology and the art of astrology. From then on, my life became unsettled and chaotic for a considerable time; my body refused to do what I wanted it to do; I often suffered from giddiness, was very restless and, for no demonstrable reason, felt stifled by my work at the university which had previously given me a great deal of pleasure. I had sizable identity problems and seemed to be going through a pretty bad period under all sorts of progressions and transits from Neptune and the ruler of my 12th house. Yet I was not really ill-starred: something was brewing, I just did not know what it was. And then, suddenly, I "knew" that I must lead a completely different life. This cut the Gordian knot. I decided to go study astrology seriously, and specifically to study astrology on a Jungian basis. In a very short space of time everything changed, from family circumstances to work, relationships and friends. I felt as if I had been reborn.

Little by little, in the years that followed, I came to realize through dreams and active imagination that any misery I suffered was caused, not by the 12th house as such, but by my lack of understanding of the way it worked. My inclination was to do everything myself, to do everything as well as possible and to honor all my commitments. Disorder and chaos were abhorrent to me—that much I had certainly discovered. In studying Jung and the workings of the mind (especially those aspects that are represented by Neptune), I delved more and more into the symbolism of dreams, myths, legends and fairy tales, and eventually came face to face with some of the problems of our Western society—seen from a Jungian point of view of course—and superbly formulated by Whitmont, among others. Our society doesn't teach us to look within. Time is money, we say, and to stand still is to go backward. Anything relating to the quietness and apparent stagnation of the 12th house wins us no immediate friends in society at large. And since "the devil finds work for idle hands," and we ought not to fiddle away our time in dreams and daydreams, the part of our psyche associated with the 12th house is pushed into a corner. No wonder we find it hard to come to terms with it!

During my internal struggles with these social values, helped as I was by dreams and visualization, I discovered more and more expressions of the 12th house that seemed to offer help rather than hindrance, and in which any initial so-called time loss through in-activity, dreaming, or occupying oneself with allegedly useless things, sometimes turned out to be time-saving because of the way the inner self developed. I am tremendously grateful for my children, too. By letting them dream and fantasize, I was able to follow them back into that story world in which symbolism, telepathy and a deep sense of the unity of life go hand in hand. Above all, I regained the ability to look at the world through the eyes of a child and to take it just as it came.

Astrology had already taught me that everything happens when its time has come; experiences and events seem always to go hand in hand with congruent progressions and transits. From Jung's psychology I learned that by changing our attitude to self and events, we take possession of a golden key for making something of life. My children showed me how to enjoy the present, without straining after any other goal; how to accept whatever comes along. In this frame of mind it is possible to perceive many subtleties that would otherwise go unnoticed. To make room for what occurs and yet remain true to ourselves seems the proper method for allowing the 12th house to deploy its great resources. These are the hidden resources that we can experience, feel, and see by means of emotion and images. In other words, the power of imagination can help us function more efficiently in the real world. In my own case, I took a journey into the unknown—into the realm of the unconscious— which at first seemed so remote and unreal, and for the first time I felt as though I had come home.

I hope to share my feelings, vision and experiences with others in this book. I have tried to paint a picture of what the possibilities are when we work consciously with the 12th house. I have worked with active imagination, and I expound on this method at some length, but there are a thousand and one other methods, all equally acceptable.

I want to thank Machiel and Machteld, our children, for all they have taught and shown me. Also, all those who participated in workshops on the 12th house in the past few years deserve my gratitude for their input and for the lively give-and-take that developed. In particular I would thank Hetty Heyster, Atie Kaper, and Corrie Kense, for allowing me to use their reports in this book. My husband Hans, who, with his emphasized 12th house and Moon in Pisces, always unerringly felt what I wanted to say, and studied the manuscript line by line, weeding out the unclear passages that I, in my enthusiasm, had overlooked. I am most grateful to him for this.

Karen Hamaker-Zondag, 1991.

Enjoyment
or
Dread?

The Twelfth House

One draws from the well without hindrance.
It is dependable. Supreme good fortune.

The well is there for all. No one is forbidden to take water
from it. No matter how many come, all find what they
need, for the well is dependable. It has a spring and never
runs dry. Therefore it is a great blessing to the whole land.
The same is true of the really great man, whose inner
wealth is inexhaustible; the more that people draw from
him, the greater his wealth becomes.[1]

All of us have the Well in us. One and all, we have deep within us
a source of wisdom, a source which supplies what we need and
never dries up. The only thing we have to do is to attend to opening
up the well and . . . to drink. Numerous experiences with the 12th
house have made it crystal clear to me that the well symbolizes this

---

[1]The I Ching, hexagram 48, top line. See Carey F. Baynes' authorized English
translation of R. Wilhelm's *I Ching*. (London: Routledge, 1983).

house, a house that is undervalued and often seen in a bad light. The I Ching says the well is there for all. In terms of Jungian psychology, we say that the deepest layer in the human psyche is that of the collective unconscious, a layer beyond time and space which binds us with life everywhere and in all times. A layer, too, in which everything originates and to which everything returns. Anyway, this part of the psyche is amply and extensively discussed by Jung and his followers. The agreement with the 12th house is striking—*if* we are prepared to notice the finer points and drop the old concept that the 12th house symbolizes nothing but misery and loss.

Time and again I have been amazed by the riches found in this house. It is a source of creativity in the art of living and, in the words of the I Ching, "is a great blessing." By falling in line with the 12th house, we add another dimension to our lives. Those who learn to listen to the inner voice will come to realize that the role of the conscious is relative and that the role of unconscious processes is vitally important for the development of the Self, as well as for a fruitful exchange between conscious and unconscious. This is the "Great Man" in us, the true Self, inexhaustibly rich in inner wealth.

Understanding the 12th house requires of us the ability to change our outlook and mode of thought. Perhaps the 12th is best described as a house of paradoxes, in which the impossible is possible and opposites can be reconciled at a deeper level—or so it seems. Its paradoxical quality is apparent, in fact, from its place in the horoscope. When the Sun rises in the east, it is astrologically speaking on the Ascendant. From this point the Sun climbs higher and higher in the heavens in the direction of the MC, and traverses the 12th, 11th, and 10th houses respectively. The 12th house has always been regarded as a veiled house, where events take place out of sight, behind shutters or behind closed doors. Such a concept is hard to reconcile with the clear light of the rising Sun, which always makes everything visible. In reality the Sun is rising, but in an astrological sense it disappears for a while when in the 12th house.

This seems contradictory: how can the Sun be visible in the sky and invisible in the chart? Nevertheless the two images *are* compatible. What we mean by this is that if we think of sunrise as a birth, the Ascendant will be the moment of coming into the world. Birth and incarnation have always been ascribed to the Ascendant, the cusp of the 1st house, the house representing the manifestation of life and vital force. Following birth there is certainly solid growth and development, but the powers of the conscious mind (the Sun) are not much in evidence at this early stage. So what is the position?

In the 12th house we find, to use the terminology of Jung, all the factors of the collective unconscious. These are the factors we carry within us as legacies from every stage of human development from the past to the present day. By calling it collective, Jung expressed the fact that it is something common to us all, regardless of sex, color, etc. The collective unconscious contains in potential all the typical human behavior patterns, just as a chemical solution contains the pattern of the crystal to be deposited. The forms themselves are not present, merely the possibility of the forms.

The fact that the Sun enters the 12th house as soon as it is visible—as soon as it crosses the Ascendant—can indicate that, from the moment of birth, the individual becomes part of a much greater heritage than the time and culture in which he or she is born. But not only this—the visible Sun moves through a secluded house where its glow is still veiled. This is nicely in accord with the view of some psychologists that the child must gradually build an ego, because the ego is not given to it readymade at birth. It sets out from virtually nothing, and does not say "I" for several years. More forcibly still, some theorists claim that human children are all premature. Erich Neumann notes in *Das Kind* (The Child) that, in comparison, the newborn of the higher mammals are much more mature than human babies.[2] To reach comparable maturity, the human embryo would have to stay in the womb for 20 through 22 months—not the nine months of normal pregnancy. Thus it takes more than a year for the human child to catch up with what the other animals were at birth. Neumann infers that the human child is an embryo not only in the womb but also during a certain post-uterine period. Portman calls this phase the social uterine time. It is a phase in which the child is already implanted in the human

---

[2]E. Neumann, *The Child* (Boston: Shambhala, 1990).

community and can grow naturally into the speech and culture of its group. The phase is characterized by the dominance of the primary relationship with the mother.

The Unconscious World

In the first year of life, the child lives in the unconscious realm and derives most of its experiences from its mother. It reacts unfailingly to her conscious and unconscious impulses, and imperceptibly learns a great deal very early on. The influence of the mother is much greater than many people think, and her behavior toward the child (which is often largely unconscious) shows the child its place. Also a number of other persons in the infant's world seem to play a key role; as, for example, its father and/or a nanny. The attitude of the mother and other key figures is the result of quite a number of factors; among which are their own characters, various problems (whether or not these have been resolved), fears, their relationships with their own parents, the part played in the cultural pattern, opinions about children derived from the culture and the society in which they live, and so on. All these are woven in a complex fashion into an attitude toward the child, but the individual is by no means always aware of it. More to the point, it seems all too often that our professed intentions toward children are different from our unconscious behavior.

Therefore, children at the breast can be pushed in a certain direction by nonverbal communication while they lie immersed in the unconscious world of either mothers or nurses. Experiences at that time may stamp powerful impressions on children. Because they have no conscious awareness of what is going on, it is very difficult in later life for them to know exactly what happened. This situation is symbolized by the Sun moving through the 12th house after rising: obviously, something is present, something is going on, but exactly what is hidden and out of reach of conscious perception. The small child is already programmed, and has already learned much, but ego-development has only just begun and has still a long way to go.

Infancy is also very important where the development of the cortex of the human brain is concerned, as may be seen from what happens in Broca's area (the speech center in the brain). See figure 1 on page 6. The density of the neurone network increases dramatically in the months following birth; thus there is a steady increase in the connections between the brain cells. Apparently when children miss out on certain experiences in their first years of life, some connections are not made. Thus in these first years a kind of base or network is prepared on which we must weave our later existence. If some of the strands are missing, then in adult life we shall experience great difficulty in making these connections.

In analytical psychology, the assumption is made that the collective unconscious is present in each of us at birth and that only later does the conscious mind develop. This has various consequences. A child is linked to its parents and to the rest of the world by its unconscious. To start with, it has no conscious, and no repression mechanism for dealing with things that are disagreeable. It is wide open, and reacts to the tensions, desires and other activities present in the unconscious of its parents. A mother who detests her child, but plays the part of a "nice kind mother," will certainly make a negative impression on it. The child invariably reacts, not to her performance in front of others, but to her repressed attitude toward it that others do not see; or, to be more precise, to the way she tenses up because of her repressed attitude toward the child.

Francis Wickes has devoted considerable space to this in her book, *The Inner World of Childhood*,[3] and Carl Jung rises to the occasion in the foreword he writes for it. He says, ". . . the things that affect children most strongly come, not from the conscious state of their parents, but from their unconscious background. This entails worry for ethically aware parents, because try as they may, the things they can more or less control, namely the conscious and its contents, seem rather ineffective in comparison with all the uncontrolled and uncontrollable background influences. Therefore it is most important for parents to study the problems of their children in the light of their own problems."

Also most important is what Jung adds on the basis of his experience. He alleges that what usually has the most powerful effect on the child's psyche is the life that the parents (and ancestors)

---

[3]F.G. Wickes, *The Inner World of Childhood: A Stud, Analytical Psychology* (Boston: Sigo Press, 1988).

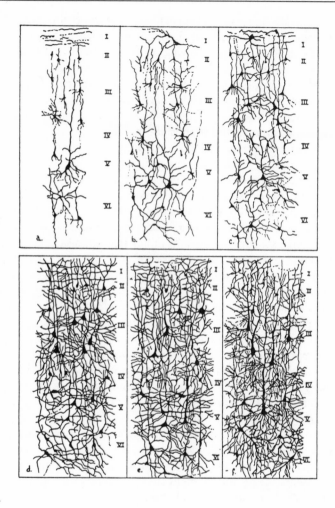

Figure 1. The 6 prepared sections of the brain show very clearly the development at a) birth, b) 1 month, c)3 months, d) 6 months, f) 24 months. In the original prepared sections the increase in density between 15 months and 24 months is greater than appears in the illustration. (From J. Leroy Conel: The Postnatal Development of the Human Cerebral Cortex.)

have not lived. Jung means by this, that part of life that the parents (and/or grandparents) would have lived if they had not "opted out" with lame excuses. In Jung's opinion, this sows the seed of serious trouble.

When meditating on the above in my study of horoscopes, I could not help thinking that the 12th house can provide some definite information on what Wickes and Jung have to say. By the 12th house I also mean the planets in that house and their aspects, and the placement of the ruler of the house together with its aspects. Even unoccupied 12th houses have rulers that can tell us much about this early phase.

I once had occasion to prepare charts for a whole family— father, mother, and three sons. The father and mother both had Mars in the 1st house: one in its own sign, Aries, the other very strongly aspected. However, Mars did not seem to be very evident in their behavior toward one another and toward others, so that it was hardly credible that the planet really was in the 1st house or so strong. They were exceptionally friendly, very obliging, and always responsive to what the world thought. They seemed so cordial, and yet . . . you felt there was something lurking in the background, although at first you could not put your finger on it. Excessive politeness and considerateness may well be a defense mechanism against personal aggressiveness, which has to be held in check at all costs lest it blazes out of control.

These parents, as I have said, had three sons; and all three experienced great difficulty in standing up for themselves. According to the father and mother, this had nothing to do with their upbringing, for—in the parents' eyes—this was reasonably free and modern. "Of course" the children had to learn to function in society, and so were assigned tasks from the time they were quite young. They had to help in the home, and were not allowed to go out to play until they had finished. They were also taught to be completely obedient to their parents. Astrologically, it was striking that all three sons had Mars in the 12th house! And that with parents who had Mars so strongly placed. Neither parent (also because of the situation in which they grew up) seems in the past to have had the courage to develop their own Mars-powers and to really learn to be themselves. They were engaged in a sort of "pious fraud." They were always ready to give way to someone else with the utmost courtesy. Behind this façade they did not need to indulge their Martian drive. But this drive would not be denied: the children were kept in a strait-jacket, while the parents had the idea that they had left them completely free. The children had to confirm the attitude of their parents, so to speak (complete obedience). This turned the parents' problem into the problem of their three sons, although in a very different form.

Thus, many times I have found problems of the parents, even problems that have descended from generation to generation, in the 12th house or in the placement of the ruler of the 12th. Often, at the birth of the child, the parents were not at all aware of any such problem, perhaps having already deeply repressed it. For example, I have seen Jupiter in the 12th in the child of a mother who had always wanted to be a student, but had never succeeded, and who settled for the life of a housewife. Or Neptune in the 12th in a child who had a parent and a grandparent with paranormal gifts who were frightened of them, or had been told by the church that such gifts were of the Devil. A whole book could be written on just all the possible forms of expression; later on we shall be looking at a few more examples.

In each case, we can find a number of 12th-house factors, linked to anxieties and repressions of the personality, which are sometimes recognizable in the family pattern and can then be ascribed to an earlier interaction with the unconscious of the parents. The 12th house and its ruler represent that part of our development that we have not undergone consciously, but through unconscious interaction has nevertheless made a powerful impression on the further development of personality and thus on that of the growth of the psyche.

The above-mentioned three sons all needed to express their Mars energy normally, but suffered from all sorts of vague and unreasoned fears when wanting to hold their own. Holding one's own is typically Martian, but the 12th house makes it difficult initially.

In this example a certain amount of stress has been laid on the anxiety that can be associated with expressions of the 12th house. Certainly, anxiety is a very frequent manifestation of the 12th house, but it is not the only one. Even less is it true that planets in the 12th or in aspect to the ruler of the 12th signify a life spent in raking up all kinds of fears. The 12th house is a source of superb expression, which often has the same origin as the fears concerning them. But this is something to be considered later. First we shall take a look at anxieties as indicated by the 12th house.

Childhood Fears

Unreality is characteristic of 12th-house fears. They seldom have roots in what the growing child has consciously experienced. Child psychology has made a number of important findings in this connection. Thus it is striking that children can be afraid of things or animals they have never seen and have no opportunity of seeing; creatures that have never frightened them by direct confrontation.

Many children say they are afraid of tigers and bears, of gorillas and other animals that they have seen at the zoo only once or twice. And the young ones are often frightened of ghosts, witches, and other mysterious and incomprehensible phenomena that have never really confronted them. Even children who are amused with stories that carefully avoid any reference to such entities and concentrate on the happy things in life, seem to have these fears!

A. T. Jersild[4] questioned a large number of children. He asked them what they were afraid of, but also what was the worst thing that had actually happened to them in their lives. Apparently, their bad experiences were sickness, pain, and the like. But they were afraid of completely different things! Frequently, they described their fears in terms of some catastrophe that might happen. The largest group, however, seems to describe those frightened of mysterious occult phenomena such as witches and ghosts. Jersild concluded that a very high proportion of all the fears described by the children had little or nothing to do with the difficulties they had encountered in everyday life.

Rollo May also has some useful comments on this theme. In his opinion, children are not afraid of "things" as such. When they are afraid of something, the cause is really an underlying general anxiety, which expresses itself in certain forms. This could explain

---

[4]A.T. Jersild, & F.B. Holmes, *Children's Fears* (Teacher's College, Columbia University, 1935).

a great number of cases in which children fear non-existent entities such as ghosts and witches. It is known that children's fears (and, all too often, those of adults as well!) are projected on witches and on things that have no direct connection with the objective world, and yet provide an important clue to the subjective needs of the children, especially in regard to their parents.

In other words, the fear expressed can mask the nature of the underlying anxiety. This also explains why children can quickly become frightened of something else when it has been made clear to them that their first fear is groundless. The external object does not matter, it is the inner state that counts!

Hagman went a step further, and researched the link between the fears of children and those of their parents, finding what seems to be a remarkable similarity, especially between the fears of the child and the fears of the mother. What is more, Jersild has discovered a noticeable agreement between the fears of children belonging to the same family. Rollo May sees in this yet another confirmation of the old adage in psychology that the development of fear in children mainly has to do with their relationship with their parents. My earlier example of the three sons who all had Mars in the 12th fits this picture well. The sons had unreasonable fears, which went hand in hand with the repressed, and therefore hidden, fears of their parents.

Fear and Saturn

The above-mentioned raises another important point. In astrology, fear is almost always associated with the planet Saturn. But fear covers a much wider territory than that belonging to Saturn. Fear is a very significant condition of the psyche; it is a state of mind that has many different forms and degrees of intensity. Thus, there is blind panic and screaming terror, so overpowering that it can lead to self-destruction (intentional or unintentional); and there is also vague uneasiness and tension. Quite often, fear is accompanied by physical sensations, also occurring in a broad spectrum. Sometimes the underlying fears are no longer observable, due to the defense mechanisms and neurotic symptoms the individual has developed.

Neurotic fears, although regarded as senseless by the outside world, mainly arise from something very real going on inside. They can be part of a defense against the threatened incursion of inner impulses that are treated as undesirable, inadmissible or evil by the culture pattern. When, through their behavior and their own fears, the parents reveal that they are suppressing certain conduct, they are signalling to their children that this conduct is bad. The danger is that the children may later develop fear or a neurosis in regard to this particular thing.

Neuroses are usually thought of in connection with the 8th house rather than the 12th, and fear in connection with Saturn. Nevertheless, experience teaches me that fear and neurosis also have a lot to do with the 12th house at times. So where does the difference lie?

Traditionally, as a psychic factor, Saturn is associated with limitation, fear and misery, and in particular with a person's secretive and unapproachable attitude in consequence of painful feelings of inadequacy and inferiority. The fact is, however, that Saturn uses life experiences to build up inner steadfastness. In doing so, it makes use of processes that help us to discover both our true strength and our limitations. Fear of new experiences that would draw us out of the shelter of our chosen restrictions is the negative side of Saturn. The reward for being bold and breaking out of these restrictions is the positive side.

Therefore fear has two faces: it can completely paralyze us, or it can stir us into action. It can be either a warning flag or a bugle call to victory. We grow by not running away from it. But, if we hang back, the result is inevitably slowing down and stagnation. The paralyzing side of fear comes in when we are scared of leaving behind the tried and trusted, of abandoning our refuge, and when we do not dare to welcome the new. Now, Saturn itself does not stand for the phenomenon of fear as such, although the assimilation, and even more so the non-assimilation of this factor in ourselves often goes with fear. It exerts an influence on all sorts of fears, and either strengthens them in a negative sense, or transcends them in a positive sense.

In a manner of speaking, Saturn is reluctant to leave behind the tried and trusted. And yet it asks from us the courage to put these things to the test and to let them die in order to make way for a new birth. However, Saturn allows plenty of time for the process; he knows nothing about hurry. When, without forcing, we are able to leave behind the old and effete, while preserving whatever is of value and taking it with us into a new phase of life, we shall be tremendously helped by the firm, structure-forming and reliable Saturn-power in ourselves. But, if we do not break free from an old attitude or situation that no longer has any value, and if we persistently fight against the necessary renewal, we shall ossify and place ourselves in opposition to the Saturn-power within us. A critical period may well ensue. Our bodies and our psyches are faced with fresh problems at the start of each new stage in life. To refuse to tackle them is to stunt our spiritual and mental growth, and it may even lead to fears, neuroses and phobias. Such fears can arise, for example, when we feel unable to rise to the challenge of the new stage.

As a psychic factor, therefore, Saturn can affect the way in which we deal with, or try to hide from, our fears, as the case may be. Since the phenomenon of fear is connected with opposition to (or incapacity for) the need for psychic growth, it is true to say that each and every psychic factor can be involved in the phenomenon. Every planet can have to do with fear in its own fashion.

Fears relating to the 12th house have to do with our earliest experiences. Usually they flow from an unconscious identification during infancy with our parents and, through them, with the collective past of our race. But also other elusive and unconsious experiences from this time can turn into fear factors; and may have, at first sight, an inexplicable influence on the native's personality and development and sphere of interests.

Of course, this earliest conditioning can (and will) occasion fine experiences, and this is something we shall look into later on. It must also be emphasized that planets in a child's 12th house do not signify that the parents have been wicked or guilty or negligent. The parents' own past has to be considered, too. They, themselves, were exposed to the unconscious influences in childhood, and have had to find ways and means of dealing with the attendant fears. However, when we are in the cradle, we are especially sensitive to unsolved conflicts or those that are avoided. But that does not mean that our parents failed during this period. On the contrary, when parents are aware (or become aware later on) of their problems and make an honorable attempt to solve them, they can give their 12th-house children such a worthwhile attitude to life, that the children can develop great gifts instead of fears. The parents will be able to appreciate the inner lives of their children, and will discover how important they are as mirrors of their own inner lives. This opens a well from which child *and* parent can drink together. But it does demand honesty from the parents and the courage to risk tripping up occasionally. The parents have to be prepared to examine themselves, to struggle with themselves, and not to blame circumstances for everything. And here we come back to the 8th house.

Fears involving the 8th house, the house of the personal unconscious, flow directly from experiences undergone in the course of our individual personality development. In the 8th house lie all sorts of experiences, desires and wishes and situations that we have forgotten, or (and the mechanism operates unconsciously) do not wish to think about, or have repressed. In one way or another, we have passed through these experiences with the developing ego. Thus they differ from the experiences of infancy. At that time, *unconscious* identification with the parents was decisive in the development of the personality, and there was no question of repression because a clearly defined ego had not yet been formed—no ego with boundaries that could say, "I will put this experience outside my boundaries, I will forget and repress it."

And so the 8th house contains not only our repressions, our forgotten experiences, but also our unconscious gifts and talents, which can rise to the surface when we solve some of our psychic problems. But the 8th and 12th houses can effectively spill over into one another. For example, if a planet in the 12th represents problems occurring in conscious life, the associated repressions and frustrations will be found in the 8th house. Many times it has seemed to me that an important progression involving the ruler of the 8th or an important transit through the 8th (especially a transit of Saturn) also throws up problems directly related to planets in the 12th or to the ruler of the 12th, even though no recognizable aspect is made in the progression or transit to these planets themselves. This shows yet again that *all* parts of the psyche are indissolubly bound up with one another.

2

A
Few
Examples

Introduction

In the previous chapter we have established that there are differences between the forms of fear ascribable to Saturn, to the 8th house, and to the 12th house. We have also established that, generally speaking, it would be unreasonable to blame people for 12th-house fears, seeing that the related factors centered in the 12th house are often those with which their parents, and possibly generations of their ancestors, have also wrestled.

We read in many astrological handbooks that when Saturn is in the 7th house, the native looks for an older partner who is by way of being a father or mother figure. But what I find in practice is that the same picture is seen with Saturn in the 12th or in aspect to the ruler of the 12th, and with Saturn in the 8th or in aspect to the ruler of the 8th (sometimes much more vividly than with Saturn in the 7th). Here are two outstanding instances from my case-book. A young lady who once visited me had Saturn in the 12th and told me that her parents' marriage had been dissolved before she was born. After some years her mother remarried. Her new father was kind and affectionate. Obviously the age difference experienced in her early years did its work, for, thanks to the good impression she retained of her step-father, she was still looking for an older, fatherly partner.

In the chart of another young lady, Saturn was prominent in the 8th. She had had a happy childhood until her 10th year. Then her parents' marriage went on the rocks. The parents stayed together, however, "for the sake of the children." The little girl and her father grew further and further apart until, in the end, she had nothing to say to him for years, even though they lived under the same roof. Obviously, this is a state of affairs likely to lead to fears and neuroses later on, especially when, as here, the father did not act with deliberate coldness toward his family. She, too, sought (and found) an older, fatherly partner.

Thus both positions of Saturn are able to produce the same external effect; in these examples the search for a father figure. But the motives and the backgrounds differ enormously. In the first girl, there were no problems in the conscious period of youth, but there was a problem situation in the last phase of fetal life and when she was a babe in arms. In the second girl there was no problem in infancy, but there was one in the conscious period of her childhood.

Here is another example. A 35-year-old woman came to consult me. She was unmarried, had a wide range of interests, but found it difficult to form a clear picture of what she really wanted to do. She was constantly torn between one thing and another and was undermining herself. Also she very often felt unsure on points where there was certainly no need to do so.

The information she gave was that she had had a happy childhood and got on well with her brothers and sisters, and that her parents loved each other dearly. Now the ruler of her 12th house was in opposition to her Ascendant and square her Sun. This is a combination that I often see associated with insecurity and identity problems connected in some way with early youthful experiences. Father, father image, and the development in which they are involved—that is to say, the development of one's own identity—are tied up with the Sun; but in a completely different manner from that in which Saturn is linked with the father theme. Saturn is more the structure and the grip on things, the Sun is more the identity.

In talking to her further, it transpired that her father was very seriously handicapped. The parents' marriage was very good, but after the birth of this daughter the mother had a very difficult time. She had been apprehensive, and had the feeling that she would have to rear the child entirely by her own efforts because her husband could do so little to help. Physically, he was in very poor shape. The burden of responsibility weighed heavily on her. She doted on her daughter, but this could not prevent the latter from sensing her anxieties, especially when the mother was nursing her. The conflict between the ruler of the 12th and the Sun is characteristic of the situation, in view of the fact that it had to do with a problem the mother had over the functioning of her husband (also represented by the Sun). There is no question here of evil intentions; quite the reverse. It was the sincerity and good intentions of the mother that formed the basis of her fears; fears which the child experienced through its unity with the mother.

An example of the fact that children are very sensitive to the unlived side in the character of their parents was that of the three sons, all of whom had Mars in the 12th. Another telling example is that of the Dutch royal family. For generations, the Dutch monarchs have been women who are also mothers. It is almost inevitable that this task—the queenship itself or the preparation for this role—with all its public obligations, should have been performed to some extent at the expense of motherhood; and we may expect it to show up in the horoscopes.

The Dutch Royal Family

Wilhelmina was born in 1880 and became queen at the age of 10, although she was not crowned until she was 18. On looking at her chart, Table 1 shows the aspects with respect to the 12th house (the charts of Juliana, Beatrix and Willem-Alexander are also summarized here in regard to their 12th house planetary factors):

Table 1. 12th House Factors.

Wilhelmina	Juliana
Co-ruler of 12 conjunct Sun	Sun in 12 conjunct ruler of 12
Ruler of 12 square Moon	Ruler of 12 trine Moon
Ruler of 12 trine Mercury	Mercury in 12
-	Venus in 12
Ruler of 12 inconjunct Mars	Ruler of 12 square Mars
-	Ruler of 12 trine Jupiter
-	-
-	-
Co-ruler of 12 trine Neptune	-
-	-

Beatrix	Willem-Alexander
Ruler of 12 square Sun	-
Ruler of 12 square Moon	Ruler of 12 opposite Moon
Co-ruler of 12 trine Mercury	-
Ruler of 12 square Venus	-
Mars in 12	Mars in 12 trine ruler of 12
Ruler of 12 square Jupiter	-
Saturn in 12	-
-	Ruler of 12 square Uranus
-	-
-	Ruler of 12 square Pluto

It is remarkable that all four members of the Dutch Royal Family, in four successive generations, have a connection between the Moon and the 12th house. The Moon symbolizes caring and cherishing, the maternal, the protective and secure. And so a connection between the Moon and the 12th house can symbolize problems that make it hard to obtain these desirable states.

These problems can be both external (for example, an upbringing restricted by convention, being left in the hands of governesses, etc.) or internal. The problems can have to do with feelings of impotence, with wondering how to fulfil the role of motherhood, becoming involved in a battle between affection and duty, a battle that brings a great sense of insecurity. There may be

the thought that the whole nation is watching how the native succeeds or fails as a mother. Another result, and one I have often
met in a link between the Moon and the 12th house, is one in
which it is not so much the mother who is unsettled, as the father.
For example, the latter may have a problem with his wife, or may
not know how to treat her in her role of mother. Also, in this
position, one of the parents may be working out a mother-problem,
either consciously or unconsciously. It is impossible to tell from
any natal chart which of these possibilities (and there are others)
might occur; but something of the sort will affect the early life of
the child born with such a link.

On examining the connections between the 4th and the 12th
house, we see that Wilhelmina (chart 1 on p. 20) has the ruler of
the 12th trine the ruler of the 4th; Juliana (chart 2 on p. 21) has
the ruler of the 12th conjunct the ruler of the 4th *and* the ruler of
the 4th in the 12th; Beatrix (chart 3 on p. 22) has the ruler of the
12th square the ruler of the 4th; and Willem-Alexander (chart 4
on p. 23) also has the ruler of the 12th square the ruler of the 4th.
Thus in four individual charts of this Royal Family, there is a connection between the Moon and the 12th house, and between the
4th house and the 12th house.

At its worst, the 4th/12th connection goes with chaos, with
the feeling of being a displaced person, with domestic disarray, with
a situation in which many members of the family travel their own
separate ways. At its best, it goes with a situation in which the
family finds help and support in its faith, or in which many artistic
activities are developed in the home (music in particular). In my
own experience, I have observed that the difficult manifestations
of a 12th/4th connection can occur with harmonious aspects such
as the trine, and that creative expressions often occur with the
disharmonious aspects. That is why, over the years, my first question
has always been whether there is in fact any aspect; only secondarily
do I check as to the nature of the aspect.

Another remarkable theme in this example is the link between
the 12th house and Mars. Wilhelmina has the ruler of the 12th
inconjunct Mars; Juliana has the ruler of the 12th square Mars;
Beatrix has Mars in the 12th; and Willem-Alexander has Mars in
the 12th and the ruler of the 12th trine Mars. Such a Mars/12th
combination often suggests that there have been problems (hered-

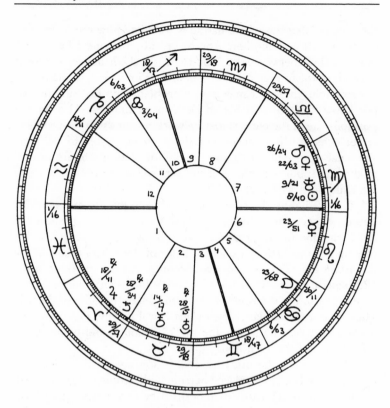

Chart 1. Natal chart for Queen Wilhelmina, born August 31, 1880, The Hague, Holland, at 6:30 P.M.

itary or environmental) in the parental (or grandparental) sphere over standing up for oneself and "doing one's own thing." Frequently, one of the parents is self-sacrificing, and sinks his or her own interests in order to keep things turning over. The need to live a personal life is suppressed; and this comes back to haunt the next generation via the 12th house. The old-fashioned concept of royalty, with all its protocol, leaves little room for freedom of expression or for following personal preference.

It is known that Beatrix originally found that being queen was completely uncongenial to her, and that is was only after long deliberation that she decided to devote herself to the role, and made up her mind that if this was something unavoidable she had to do, then she would do it well. The surrender of part of her needs-pattern, the more provocative and undermining part (Aquarius with many Uranus conflicts and an Aries Ascendant!) may be traced again in the Mars/12th combination in her eldest son, who is likely to be just as impatient at having his freedom of movement restricted.

It is noteworthy that his mother's provocative side is repeated in Willem-Alexander's 12th house: he has the ruler of the 12th square Uranus. In the earlier generations there are no connections between the 12th house and Uranus or, for that matter, between the 12th house and Pluto. On the other hand, Willem-Alexander

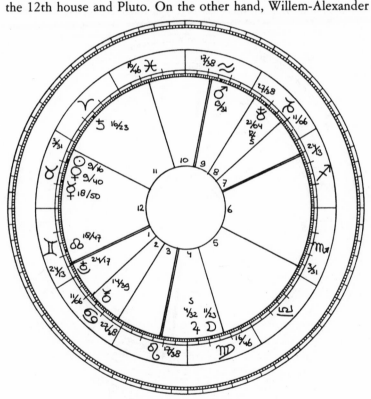

Chart 2. Natal chart of Juliana, born April 30, 1909, The Hague, Holland, at 6:50 A.M.

has no connections between the 12th house and the Sun, Mercury and Venus; connections which were prominent in the charts of his mother, grandmother and great-grandmother. Beatrix and Claus wished to give their children a modern upbringing, and they tried to allow them as much freedom as was possible in the circumstances. But in spite of their best endeavors, the heir to the throne was still saddled with an inherited 12th/Moon combination and a 12th/4th combination.

Another point of interest, is that Beatrix has Saturn in the 12th house. This is a very common placement for someone with a father figure who, for some reason or other, did not function adequately for the child (or even was completely absent). As we know, Beatrix

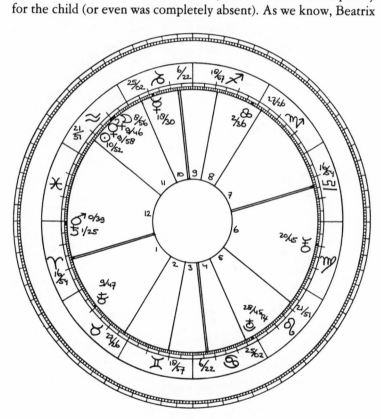

Chart 3. Natal chart for Beatrix, born January 31, 1938, Soestdijk, Holland, at 9:47 A.M.

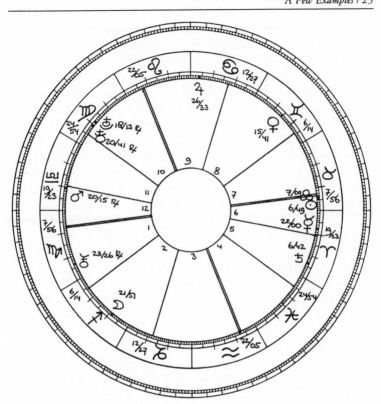

Chart 4. Natal chart of Willem Alexander, born April 27, 1967, Utrecht, Holland, at 7:57 P.M.

was born just before the outbreak of World War II, and her mother Juliana took refuge in Canada, together with Beatrix and her sister Irene who was born in 1939. Her father, Prince Bernhard, remained behind. Therefore the two little sisters did not have the presence of their father in a normal family unit during their first years. (The 12th house covers the whole mythic phase—roughly the first seven years, but the first four years of this period are very important). It is worth mentioning that Princess Irene also has Saturn in the 12th house!

From this example it can be seen how sometimes many generations may be affected by the same problem, but also that problems involving the 12th house can have to do with unavoidable circumstances at the time of birth or during the first few years of life. That these circumstances are occasionally out of the ordinary, is well shown by the following example. I once received a phone call from an astrological colleague when I was preparing a workshop on the 12th house, and we had a discussion about his own 12th house. Mercury and Venus occupied the 12th house and the ruler of the 12th was inconjunct the Sun. He related that, as far as his early years were concerned, he had been born in a haunted house, a house in which all sorts of inexplicable phenomena occurred! His parents had many tales to tell about it, some of them gruesome, and some of them rather comic. These experiences left their mark on him. He remained extremely sensitive to this kind of thing and, in spite of a down-to-earth outlook on the world, he said that he also heard and saw other things, things that obviously belong to "another world." He was more sensitive than many people, was sometimes regarded as strange, and was frequently misunderstood. In addition to his everyday work, he devoted himself to philosophical and metaphysical problems, with occultism and magic, and developed a very individual point of view on these subjects. He himself thought that the early association with a haunted house had contributed to his outlook.

I like telling this story, because it illustrates that we are not always dealing with the reaction of a child to its mother or with the child's relationship with its parents. As far as the collective unconscious is concerned, the child is part of its whole living environment, and it reacts to the latter. Of course, there are not too many of us who can say we were born in a haunted house; and so our unconscious participation in parental circumstances are the usual basis of early 12th-house experiences.

With the last example, we have broken fresh ground, which also has to do with the 12th house—the world of the paranormal and the unseen. The psychiatrist Jan Ehrenwald has disclosed, in superb fashion, that the paranormal is involved in the early parental situation. But that is a topic we shall have to leave for the next chapter.

3

The
Parent-Child
Symbiosis

Extrasensory Perception

As we have seen, the small child, even while lying as a helpless baby in its cradle, participates in its surroundings by means of the unconscious of its mother. It lies, so to speak, completely imbedded in her psyche—ideal conditions for telepathic communication between them. The literature of parapsychology often emphasizes the frequent occurrence of telepathy between parent and child, and especially between mother and child. The researches of E. Spinelli in England (1976) have made clear that young children of three and four score very highly in tests for extrasensory perception, whereas the scores of adolescents and adults are significantly lower. Generally speaking, the telepathic link gets weaker as the child grows older. The child detaches itself from its parents in order to develop its own ego, and the unconscious connection gradually loses its vital function and activity.

In *The ESP Experience: A Psychiatric Validation,*[5] Jan Ehrenwald

---

[5]J. Ehrenwald, *The ESP Experience: A Psychiatric Validation* (Annual convention of the Parapsychological Assn., New York, 1978).

supplies a valuable commentary on this process. He puts forward the hypothesis that, owing to the symbiosis of mother and child, the mother through her psyche may release certain behavior in the child: certainly when the child is very young. He thinks it not impossible that it is a sense of purpose emanating from the mother's psyche that summons the smile to the baby's face, not an impulse from the baby itself. This may seem like a back-to-front way of looking at the world, But Ehrenwald supports it with, among other things, his observation that mentally handicapped children sometimes function remarkably better when their mothers are with them, and especially when the mothers are eager that the children achieve something. It is as if a child "reads" unconsciously the answers to questions from the unconscious of its mother, with whom it is so closely tied. If this is what happens, then it is not the child who gives the answer, but the mother who gives it unconsciously via the child.

Telepathy, continues Ehrenwald, is in fact the embryonic matrix (maternal milieu) for the imparting of information, a function that is later taken over by speech. (Speech, which distinguishes clearly defined things, depends on the presence of a separate ego.) How many parents have not discovered that they usually knew or felt what was the matter with their child? Obviously, this type of telepathic contact between parent and child is usually necessary because, although the infant is in a sort of post-embryonal phase, it is as thoroughly helpless in comparison with the young of other higher mammals as if it were still "unborn." Only after nine months through a year, does it start to "get going."

But the child soon outstrips the animals. It learns to talk, as the ego begins to form and demarcate itself. Slowly the symbiosis (the common life) with the mother is broken. The child becomes an independent unit. It builds its own identity, apart from that of the mother, and even puts up barriers in order not to have the process disturbed by the psyche of the mother (or father). It is no longer completely part of her (his) psychic world, but makes one for itself. This is an extremely important operation in the life of the child.

At the same time, telepathic communication begins to decrease, and it seems that the child also erects barriers to ward off disturbing influences that might reach it by this route. By doing so, it helps the development of its own personality to take place as peacefully as possible. Ehrenwald makes it clear that children who do *not* take this step run a greater risk of developing schizophrenic reactions or even forms of autism. It is worth noting that Ehrenwald has carried out his psychiatric investigations in a culture in which, until a short time ago, everything to do with the paranormal was regarded as a nonsense, was denied, and was pushed to one side. For this reason, children who remain open to telepathic processes refrain from talking about them. This is something we learn from the life histories of many psychics.

Thus, at a given moment, the child breaks free from the unconscious of the mother and, in a certain sense, we can speak of this as a birth. Birth in the ordinary sense, the physical separation of mother and child, becomes a fact with the severing of the umbilical cord. The psychic birth, a few years later, as soon as the child has reached a certain point in the development of its own identity, can be seen as the cutting of a psychic umbilical cord. This time it is the child itself who does the deed, and only then does it stand on its own feet. It has become self-conscious and starts developing on this basis. Consciousness of the ground in which it takes root will not come until much later, when it has discovered the range of its inner possibilities. But through this first step of independence the child loses the original predominating connection with its collective background, just as in its physical birth it lost its warm nest in the amniotic fluid in the mother's womb. Yet although telepathic ability gradually lapses into a latent possibility, it does not disappear.

PSI and Astrology

So how can we place this in the context of astrology? We have seen that infancy, the time of symbiosis with the mother, lies in the 12th house. This, if we follow the line laid down for us by Ehrenwald, should be found to play a large part in paranormal processes. From the study of the charts of some tens of individuals with paranormal gifts, I have come to the conclusion that, next to the planet Neptune, the 12th house and the ruler of the 12th play a very important role. The psychics whose horoscopes I have studied have all taken part in experiments supervised by various university parapsychology units, so that we do not need to doubt their talents. In their charts, one of the main features is the conflicting aspects between Neptune and the ruler of the 12th. It is natural to suppose that something went wrong with the cutting of the psychic umbilical cord. By "went wrong" I chiefly mean that the development of a personal ego (or of one part of it) by the child took a different course from the usual one. The child remained sensitive to influences from outside which, at their most negative, can undermine the conscious mind and then form a danger to the development of the personality. But, more positively, the child, and later the adult, can participate in the environment with such deeply rooted involvement that, without the use of words, it knows much, experiences much, sees much and foresees much.

This alternative development, when something goes wrong, can have many causes. If the child is going to sever the psychic umbilical cord, there must be a psychic umbilical cord to sever. In other words, to put it simply, there must be a link with the mother. When the mother is absent and there is no reliable foster parent, when there is loneliness, or no contact or at least no emotional involvement by the parents, then, when the time comes, the child will have no idea of the break it would normally make; and there is a big chance that it will stay closely connected to the collective unconscious, and preserve an unusual sensitivity to subliminal and non-verbal impressions and signals.

It is a psychological truism that many paragnosts, clairvoyants and sensitives have had a difficult time in youth. The early years of the psychometrist Croiset were beset by chaotic circumstances. Later he never stayed long in any place, and he was often alone. But even those psychics who were blessed with a good home in their formative years, and therefore should have been able to see what had to be severed, seem to have suffered traumas that prevented normal development of the psyche. The famous Russian medium Nina Kulagina, for example, knew terrible deprivation in her early years during the aftermath of the revolution, and very nearly starved to death.

Other celebrities, such as Uri Geller and Matthew Manning, to name two, had traumatic experiences in early childhood also. Actual harm, privation, difficulties, tensions, etc., whether or not due to the parents' fault, are found—if they occurred in early childhood—in the 12th house and in the aspects made by the ruler of the 12th.

A very dominant mother, who gives her child no room to move, sometimes because of her own psychic problems, can (generally unconsciously) prevent her child from cutting the psychic umbilical cord. Ehrenwald calls such mothers "the witches of our time." He also places in the same context the fact that children can indulge in the very things that were repressed or unconscious in their parents. Even that is a form of telepathy that fits nicely into the 12th house. Ehrenwald, and other psychiatrists/parapsychologists, very often mention the bond with the mother. However, some researchers state that the father, and indeed others who look after the child on a regular basis, can play a similar part, and that the father in particular can make an impression on the child through the unconscious of his wife (with whom he is united both consciously and unconsciously). On the basis of my more than fifteen years' experience with the 12th house, I feel I can safely say that the parts played by the father and the mother are equal where the 12th house of the child is concerned.

In short, the 12th house represents our connection with the collective unconscious, by means of which we are linked with everything and everybody, in a dimension outside of time and space. Yet within the collective unconscious, it is the unconscious of our parents to which we react most. We participate in the world via their unconscious. But, if we are not to endanger the growth of our conscious minds and of our egos (and therefore that of our personalities), we must break free from this (unconscious) tie—at least to a great extent. However, as I have already said, the cutting of the psychic umbilical cord means that we are largely shut off from our collective origin and from nature in ourselves.

On the other hand, if the cord is not severed, then we remain all our life long closely connected with everything and everybody. Our connection with the collective unconscious can reveal itself in countless different ways. But it is important to bear one thing in mind, and that is that the forms in which it reveals itself certainly need not be negative, as we shall see by and by.

Those with a black-and-white approach to astrology regard the 12th house as the "house of loss," and say it is preferable not to have any planets in it, since they would be nothing but a source of misery. They add that whatever these planets might promise would fail, or would bring a peck of troubles. According to them, the unfortunate native might be jailed or institutionalized. All this, and more, they pour on the wretched heads of people unlucky enough to have 12th-house planets.

Happily, a different picture is seen in practice, and the doom and gloom seldom or never comes true. As for the so-called loss, well that depends on one's viewpoint. The 12th house is impenetrable; admittedly, it is difficult to assess, and its contents are concealed from the conscious mind like a landscape shrouded in mist. But are we justified in calling this a loss? Of course, our conscious minds seek tangible, clear-cut facts. We want to keep a firm grip on affairs. And, of course, the 12th house is not going to oblige us; of that we may be sure. To do so would be out of character. However, it does not follow that everything involved in this house is a write-off—far from it! The planets there may lie slumbering; but, at a certain moment, they will bestow something that, although it may be hard to describe, is vitally important.

Because 12th-house planets have to do with the unbreakable and unconscious link between the world about us and our inner being, we can effectively help ourselves by communicating via this link in a way that by-passes the conscious. More than once, I have seen individuals with many 12th house planets tune in unerringly on latent social trends; and, hardly realizing what they are doing, steal a march on all the rest who are trying to analyze future tendencies by means of logic, statistics and market research. Well, the 12th-house folk did just one thing: they were able to listen to something within themselves, and without giving it a second thought they obeyed the inner prompting, not realizing the full significance of what they were doing. Naturally, they reaped their reward. Thus, I am reminded of the publisher who, acting on an apparent whim, decided "out of the blue" to bring out a book on a certain subject. The subject was one that, at the time, seemed to be arousing not the slightest interest. And what happened? At the time the book came out there was a television program on that very subject, and the volume was instantly in great demand. The publisher knew nothing about the preparations being made for the television program, and therefore nothing about the effect this was likely to have on his publication. He simply followed a hunch.

Time and life stream, as it were, through these people. In a positive sense, they are able to give shape to the future, subtly but unmistakably. They are, and remain, bound up with the timeless and spaceless collective unconscious, which also contains the dormant future. When they surrender themselves to this indefinable, inaccessible source of inspiration, they are able to give expression to what is going to become important in the months ahead. Also they know infallibly how to act on others, without theorizing about it; like the musician who instinctively feels how the audience will respond to his playing, and performs in such a way that they are enraptured. By nature, the house is indefinable, but whoever takes it on its own terms can derive incalculable benefit from it. Least of all, should we think of it as a disadvantage. On the contrary, a heavily tenanted 12th house could presage great material success!

4

The
General Effect
of 12th House Planets

Duality

The 12th house is, and always will be, a veiled house, a house symbolizing links with the unconscious, and especially with the collective unconscious. Planets in this house and in aspect to the ruler of the 12th represent sensitive areas that are the result mainly of our unconscious interaction with our surroundings in general, and with our parents in particular during the so-called mythic phase, covering approximately the first six or seven years of childhood. As we have already seen, the earliest years of this period are of decisive importance.

Planets in the 12th and in aspect with the ruler of the 12th, because of their sensitivity, tend to make us turn inward. They can give deep insight into or grasp of all those matters or processes that swamp the individual, and of the collective and universal. But where the things for which they stand have to be given form in the world of the concrete, these planets often land us in problems, at least initially. They have much to contribute to our life in the outside world, but only after certain difficulties have been overcome or a different attitude has been learned.

Because of the vulnerability associated with these psychic factors, we are shy about mentioning them when we are children, and avoid any situation where they would be brought out into the open. It is not unusual for the parents, other relatives, or other people in the child's environment, to make it clear that speech or behavior belonging to planets in the 12th or in aspect to the ruler of the 12th are undesirable. This can be done by prohibitions and punishments; but much more often there is an ambiguous attitude on the part of those around toward these factors, so that the child feels insecure concerning them. Or the attitude of the parents and other adults betrays obvious disapproval, although with their mouths they profess not to mind. Now it is just this ambiguity that has the most powerful formative effect on planets in the 12th or in aspect to the ruler of the 12th. For they react not so much to what people pretend, as to the real motives behind their words. They enable the native to know infallibly if word and deed are in agreement.

Rollo May throws a very illuminating light on this discrepancy. In his book *The Meaning of Anxiety*,[6] he reports a piece of research on thirteen unmarried mothers regarding the connection between neurotic fears and rejection by the parents. His remarkable conclusion is that it is not so much outright rejection that later gives rise to neurotic fears as rejection that hides itself under professions of love and care. In other words, the child reacts unfailingly to the real, unconscious message that says, "You are rejected," or, "You are not accepted," and is unable to reconcile it with the apparent outer reality fabricated by spurious attention and meaningless gifts.

When the situation described by Rollo May arises in the more conscious time of youth, the contents of the 4th house play a rather important part. But the basis is laid in the 12th house. The ambiguous attitude, especially in the first few years, can prevail without the parents, nurses and others being aware of it. This can be the case when we are dealing with a "pious-lie" as Jung named it; but I have frequently observed that planets in the 12th or in aspect to the ruler of the 12th have to do with generations lying further back. The child is always a twig on the family tree, and the family history sits somewhere in the child. In many instances, that "somewhere"

---

[6] Rollo May, *The Meaning of Anxiety* (New York: Washington Square Press, a division of Simon & Schuster, 1979).

is the 12th house it seems. Thus planets in the 12th or in aspect to the ruler of the 12th can represent the struggles of the parents, which were the consequence of the struggles of their own parents (the child's grandparents) and so on.

But, one way or another, the ambiguous behavior it encounters can fill the child with anxiety when it comes to expressing the things represented by planets in the 12th or in aspect to the ruler of the 12th. It feels unable to come to terms with them, is very insecure in the areas covered by the planets and runs the risk of falling into difficulties in these areas, because its fear induces it to repress or ignore them. Therefore it can not handle them properly in conscious life; and it is quite likely that such factors will express themselves in a more primitive and more trying manner. Nevertheless, this situation need not be permanent, among other reasons because, if we open up, it is always possible to bring the factors into play normally.

To conclude, we can say that with planets in the 12th or in aspect to the ruler of the 12th, we have to reckon with the following:

• We can be charged with feelings of fear or guilt (though not always);

• We may find difficulty in expressing what we represent;

• We feel that we have little or no grip on the things they represent;

• We are inclined to construct defense mechanisms against the things they represent, or to take evasive action against them;

• The factors involved are sensitive or vulnerable spots.

An unaspected ruler of the 12th is a special case. As it has no direct links with other planets, there are none that display specific 12th-house forms of expression as described above. However, such an unaspected ruler of the 12th is, in practice, very sensitive to the things mentioned—sometimes to the extent that its main characteristics are uncertainty, side-stepping and vulnerability. An unaspected planet tends to make a big impact on the way in which the horoscope works out. Quite often, we see that much of the horoscope is colored by an unaspected planet.

Children born with an unaspected ruler of the 12th often experience in their mythic phase something disagreeable or hard to understand, a source of great insecurity. In a number of cases this has had to do with breast-feeding. At various times I have met a mother who fed her baby at the breast and had what she thought was a warm and loving relationship with it. But the child did not thrive, and it cried a lot. From the mother's point of view there appeared to be no problems, and the flow of milk was good. However, after some months, it was realized that the nutrient level was too low, so that the child had suffered from hunger. Supplementary feeding with the bottle (or by giving small amounts of solids) quickly overcame the problem. For the mother, this was invariably a shocking experience, especially if the problem had not arisen with her previous children and if she was not aware of its existence. Unintentionally, her darling child had been given a very bad start in life, with hunger, crying and a lack of understanding of its trouble. That such a precarious beginning (think of the connections being made between the brain cells!) can affect the unconscious far into adult life, goes without saying.

Also I have come across children with an unaspected ruler of the 12th, whose parents had had to face in the children's first years that the life they had led had caused them to grow apart, and this kept the parents busy trying to patch up their differences. In many instances, the period in question was a painful time, psychologically as well as in other ways. In other instances, just as with the Sun or Moon in the 12th, there has been hospitalization, either of the child itself or of one of the parents, or else a very traumatic experience involving a small brother or sister that has upset the parents so much that for a while they have functioned on automatic pilot so to speak. I can think of the case of a little girl whose brother died of a children's disease when she was only a year old.

Thus an unpleasant or tragic situation affecting the emotional life and the sense of security is characteristic of an unaspected ruler of the 12th. However, such situations are not necessarily permanent. Parents do sometimes manage to resolve quite serious differences; also infant feeding problems are usually overcome. Nevertheless, the child preserves residual effects of the experience (to which the unaspected ruler of the 12th has made it extra sensitive) and comes out of it with increased vulnerability. So far, I have not met with an unaspected ruler of the 12th that was not attended by early problems: though I would not entirely rule out the possibility that I might do so one day. To some extent, these problems add a flavoring of uncertainty and vulnerability to all the other chart factors.

But, coming back now to planets in the 12th or in aspect to the ruler of the 12th, we find that, with these planets, we tend to become involved in the very situations that our conscious minds plan to dodge. The situations are apparently like magnets; so that we are repeatedly confronted with what we are desirous to avoid. The stronger our defense mechanism, the more painful this is.

Interestingly enough, the 12th house is reputedly the house of secret enemies; and, to start with, we fail to recognize that the 12th-house factors belong to ourselves, and that we are projecting them on the outside world. Because we project them without knowing what we are doing, it is easy to lay blame on others, attributing to them all sorts of hidden motives and missing our own involvement. In fact we remain our own hidden enemies as long as we do not realize what the other side of the 12th house has to offer.

The gift of attracting certain situations unintentionally has a rather unexpected feature. With planets in the 12th or in aspect to the ruler of the 12th, people can find themselves in situations they have not consciously sought. Such situations can be difficult to escape from and yet, strangely enough, they may turn out to be very agreeable. Thus, people with Mercury in the 12th can engage in trade, writing, journalism, publishing or bookselling, without consciously choosing to do so, or even rather against their will. But this need not be a disaster; in fact, it may give a lot of pleasure. The crux of the matter is that the people feel that life has dumped them somewhere and left them to make the best of it, but it has all turned out well in the end. This is the good side of the 12th house: if these people let things come as they may, it seems they will often be led to do things that promote their best interests. If they are in business, say, they may unintentionally stock up with the very line that is going to sell well.

Nevertheless, business people, such as I described in my example, will feel that they are not managing their Mercury-in-the 12th factor as they would like. And here we have one of the marks of planets in the 12th or in aspect to the ruler of the 12th: it is hard to control their conscious expression, and this gives the natives a sense of searching. The latter can show itself in two ways: either the natives unconsciously seek situations in which they must give form to the factor, however unsure they are of it initially, or else the natives seek situations in which the factor can be completely ignored, and so becomes dependent on others or on the environment. A middle way is generally found, but usually these people have to live and learn first.

Because we have no grasp in the ordinary way of planets in the 12th or in aspect to the ruler of the 12th, we sometimes prefer to express the factors involved when we are on our own. But, as might be expected, even so we tend not to be aware that we are expressing them in this form. Therefore planets in the 12th or in aspect to the ruler of the 12th often give good indications of what an individual is likely to do when he or she is alone. Strange as it may seem, although the 12th house has the reputation of being the house of loneliness, people with many planets in the 12th are hardly ever bored. The same applies to people with many planets in aspect to the ruler of the 12th. Such people are often very busy when they are on their own, for their uncertainty—which they feel toward the outside world—has been shut outside. Look at people with Mars in the 12th, for example, and see how energetically they work when left to themselves.

One result of planets in the 12th house or in aspect to the ruler of the 12th can be that, because of our insecurity and lack of grip on the factors concerned, we run the risk of being easily hurt or nervous over these factors, and of creeping into our shell. We try to keep these factors to ourselves as much as possible; but what we fail to observe is that we are so preoccupied with them on the quiet that others find the whole thing very frustrating. For instance; with the Moon in the 12th or in aspect to the ruler of the 12th, we are very sensitive emotionally, and it costs us a lot to express our emotions freely. At the same time, our emotions and moods can place a heavy burden on those around us, who find us unbalanced at times, or meddlesome, or attention-grabbing, etc. We ourselves are scarcely ever or never aware of this. Yet, only when we can trace the trouble back to our own attitudes, shall we appear more stable to those around us.

When our vulnerability makes it hard to give direct expression to planets in the 12th or in aspect to the ruler of the 12th, it is easier to express them indirectly, or in a form where there is no personal relationship. For example, people with the Moon or Venus in the 12th often find it difficult to display feelings of warmth and tenderness, however much they may long to do so. They want to wait until the time and place are right; and, if the time and place are not right, they suffer from inhibition. Their sensitivity makes them clam up—the sensitivity is hidden away, but we may depend on it that it is there all right. In fact, the sensitivity is so great with planets in the 12th or in aspect to the ruler of the 12th that the expression of any personal regard is next to impossible. Yet the native readily identifies with the emotions of others; and this gives the rather contradictory picture of someone who avoids close contacts and yet has to fight back the tears when the news of some disaster is broadcast on TV. Problems will obviously exist in the sphere of personal living, but at the same time there is the possibility of extending a helping hand through, for example, charitable organizations.

The interest in others, and the sympathy with their sorrows and sufferings, produces born social workers and outstanding relief workers. These people generally have a great need to stand up for the poor, the oppressed and the outcast. Relief work, social service, development programs, nature conservancy, animal protection, the rehabilitation of drug addicts, organizing shelter for the homeless, aid to refugees, and so on, are areas in which people with a prominent 12th house feel in their element. There they can release the emotions that are so easily bottled up in personal relationships. The knowledge that their sympathies are being harnessed for the good of others, and that the kindness shown will reap its reward, can be a step in the direction of growing self-confidence. With this encouragement, it should be possible to express the factors represented by planets involved in the 12th house in a better and more direct way.

Sacrifice

The 12th house has always been seen as the house of sacrifice, the house in which we deny ourselves on behalf of a higher ideal. But it also carries the threat of disassociation, liquidation of the personality and the loss of all hold on reality. These aspects are, in fact, traceable to a single need, the need to experience unity. The 12th house expresses, as I have already said, our link with the collective unconscious, the layer in the psyche where we are united with everything and everyone in a wider life. This is the layer that knows neither time nor space and where everything coexists in an Eternal Now, impossible though this may seem to the conscious mind. It is certainly possible to experience the sense of unity, even though it can not be thought of rationally or conveyed in words. It comes to each of us at certain moments, and does so unmistakably; being most real and convincing to those with Pisces, Neptune, or the 12th house strong in their charts. In the collective unconscious, we are one with the world, one with the past and one with the future. Somewhere inside us is a longing to experience unity and union with the conscious mind, so that being on our own no longer means being lonely but allows us to relive that communion with all and everything that we unconsciously enjoyed in infancy.

In experiencing this connection with the roots of our individual existence, we find that it no longer matters whether we are helping others or ourselves, for we are all one. And so in its positive effects the tendency to sacrifice displayed by the 12th house does not lead to liquidation of the personality, but rather to giving form to the collective in us in a very personal manner. For example, these people can make it their life's work to help the third world, or can retreat to the cloister for a life of inner contemplation or can engage in some other form of religious activity.

Nevertheless, the need to experience the underlying unity does have its dangers. Intoxication with drink or drugs can give for a time the illusion of participation in a greater whole, or can blur the sense of personal limitations so that we feel free. But it is not a real liberation that they give, it is not the achievement of the ability to experience unity and a love for the whole with a deeper understanding. Therefore the temporary sense of freedom can become enslaving, and therefore all addictions come under the 12th house.

Now alcoholism and drug addiction are not generally regarded as socially acceptable, but they are not the only forms of addiction found under the 12th house, which covers every addiction that undermines the personality. Thus one can fall under the spell of cults that demand that their members give up everything for them, or subject their recruits to brainwashing. But some people are actually slaves to socially acceptable—even highly regarded—qualities such as self-sacrifice. They are always at the beck and call of others and day and night they are ready to help. Very noble, of course; but when this represents an avoidance of making something of oneself, a refusal to take proper responsibility for one's own life, and an inability to act differently, then it becomes as undermining as any other form of addiction.

The 12th house knows all sorts of ways of helping people to run away from themselves before they are aware of it. This explains why instability and the inclination to clutch at unworkable Utopian ideas or other forms of unreality also belong to the 12th house. By its very nature, the 12th house is unrestrained. Thus whether the individual is addicted to self-sacrifice, to blind devotion to some "ism," or to drink, the selfsame process lies at the bottom of it, namely denial of self due to a false sense of unity.

The connection with the unseen world is exceptionally strong in the 12th house. For convenience sake, I lump under the heading "unseen world" all those things we can not rationalize or often explain, but which can nevertheless play an important part in our lives. Just to dip into the subject here and there, we can offer as examples religious emotions, cosmic consciousness, extrasensory perception, working with (still) unexplained energies and psychic powers, dreams, hypnotism, meditation, symbolism, the world of myths, legends and fairy tales, creative imagination, etc., etc. These things all come under the 12th house; and planets in the 12th and in aspect to the ruler of the 12th seem to be outstanding instruments for them. This brings us to a very creative side of the 12th house: it hands us the means (at first, no more than a latent possibility) of adding another dimension to our lives. Then, even in times of adversity, we can find the help and support, either from within or from without, required in order to survive. Here, too, the experience of unity has a part to play, as we shall see further on.

Certainly, in an objective sense, the unseen world is not very concrete; yet we can make good use of it in everyday living. To handle it creatively we have to take a step in the direction of the 12th house. We must prepare the right conditions. These will be explained in detail in a later chapter.

5

Fate
and the
12th House

The Chicken or the Egg (Which Came First?)

The following is taken from a student's report: "I was born during
the Second World War. When my mother was carrying me she
suffered from panic fears whenever there was a bombing raid. When
she heard the approach of enemy aircraft she became completely
hysterical. I have a conjunction of the Moon and Pluto in my 12th
house, and the Moon is also ruler of the 12th. I myself am over-
sensitive to sound. It makes me nervous, and I get very uptight if
others are noisy. If the neighbors are playing loud music, I become
obsessed, and it can drive me to distraction."

Each workshop on the 12th house I have conducted has
brought experiences such as these to light, experiences that confirm
my opinion that we can find in the 12th house not only the mythic
phase of the child, but also the last phase of the period in the womb,
and possibly the whole embryonic phase.

The investigations of Dr. Thomas H. Verny and John Kelly
have proved that prenatal experiences can go on exerting an effect
far into adulthood, even though we remember nothing of them. In

their book, *The Secret Life of the Unborn Child*,[7] they give a number of telling examples. One of these concerns a man who suffered from severe anxiety attacks coupled with fits of temper. He consulted the West German physician Dr. Paul Bick, a pioneer in hypnotherapy. Dr. Bick put his patient into a trance and regressed him to the time when he was in the womb. Under hypnosis, he calmly related all sorts of events from this period, until he came to the seventh month of prenatal life. Then he became panicky and his voice sounded strained. He was flushed and nervous. It was obvious to Dr. Bick that something must have happened that was bringing on anxiety attacks and fits of temper in adult life. This trauma that occurred in the seventh month was eventually revealed by the mother in a long and painful interview—in that month she had tried to terminate her pregnancy by taking scalding hot baths.

But there are also happier experiences. Mothers who during their pregnancy have kept singing or humming a certain lullaby to the baby, will be astonished to find after the birth that, when it is peevish, this lullaby will have a nearly magical effect and will calm the child almost instantaneously. It will also respond to the father's voice if he has bent down and spoken and sung to the child at regular intervals during the pregnancy. Verny and Kelly believe there is good reason to suppose that the seeds of a number of our interests and fears are sown in this early period. Astrologically, of course, there is still no birth chart. The birth chart itself is waiting to be "born" along with the child.

Sooner or later in our researches we arrive at the classic "chicken or the egg" situation. Since planets in the 12th or in aspect to the ruler of the 12th can provide information about experiences in the mythic phase of the child, and also about areas the parents have found sensitive during the last phase of the pregnancy, it looks as if the horoscope is already active before the child enters the world. The question is, are we born with a certain horoscope because of the situation in which we find ourselves, or are our experiences decided by the nature of the chart? Lectures and workshops are frequently held on this subject, and the questions posed run something like this: if the horoscope represents what happens to us, how can it say anything about what our parents did

---

[7]T.R. Verny & J. Kelly, *The Secret Life of the Unborn Child* (New York: Dell, 1982).

not do? When we encounter problems that were encountered by our parents, is that due to some form of predestination? Or do our parents' problems favor a time of birth for us that will get these problems into our charts? Or are certain problems simply inherited? What about premature or induced births? And how do adopted children fit into the picture?

These are difficult questions. For one thing, we are now bordering on the region where our philosphy of life, our beliefs and our convictions play a part. Some will refer to karma as the answer, but others find karma and reincarnation unacceptable or too far-fetched. It is not my plan to enter into the dispute; however, turning aside from that, it is useful to note that a horoscope, strictly speaking, is nothing more than a "blueprint of the heavens for a given moment." The horoscope can be that of a calf, or a business decision; it does not have to be the chart of a human birth. The horoscope itself does not tell us that it has to do with an individual, therefore care should be taken when trying to interpret it. And so I shall confine myself to using some examples from my practice. Readers can then fit these examples into their own beliefs or philosophies of life.

If experiences during the last months in the womb can be found in the 12th house, together with unconscious factors of the parents, the unconscious environment, etc., we can then make the cautious assumption that the horoscope is somehow operative before birth. Experiences with my own children have strengthened my conviction that this is so. When I was carrying my first child, the midwife calculated the date of birth as the 20th of September, which would have made him a Virgo. From the moment I knew I was pregnant, I made a note of every significant event; even phone calls from well-wishers who had heard I was expecting. The amazing thing was how often during the first three months the MC or Ascendant in the chart of such a phone call or chat about the baby etc., aspected something in my horoscope. My radical Ascendant and radical Pluto kept coming to the fore. In other words, nearly always, when the conversation turned on the coming child, one of the four angles of that moment (AC, DC, MC, or IC) was conjunct with or in other aspect to my radical AC or radical Pluto. Less often, another factor in my chart was aspected. Thus, in the first three months, it was my horoscope that played a role.

This changed in the course of the fourth month. From that moment onward, the Aries/Libra and the Leo/Aquarius axes were very often on the angles, not only when we were engaged in thinking about the child (e.g., choosing a name, discussing the context of the birth chart) but also when concrete things happened, such as the purchase of a pram or the ordering of birth announcement cards. And when it kicked in the womb, these two axes were prominent. In a number of cases, practically the same degree—10 - 11 Aries or Libra or the last degrees of Leo or Aquarius—was at the top of the chart of the event in question. No wonder we began to suspect that our child would be born somewhat later than the calculated date, and would not be a Virgo but a Libra. It was funny, but the typeface that appealed to us most for the birth announcements was called Libra! At last the baby was born: a son with the Sun at 11° Libra and an Ascendant in Aquarius at the end of the sign.

We had the same experiences with our second child. Here, again, especially in the first months, there were points of contact with my own horoscope (once more with the Ascendant and Pluto) and changes around the fourth month. However, with this child, my rising sign very often put in an appearance even after the fourth month. The birth was calculated for the 18th of February, which is an Aquarian birth date, but my Ascendant is Pisces.

Our daughter is a Pisces—so it was not my Ascendant that kept cropping up, but her Sun sign! In addition, the Cancer/Capricorn axis occurred in the horary charts with surprising frequency, and the last degrees of these signs were much in evidence. As I suffered considerably from gravidic sciatica during this pregnancy (a debilitating nerve pain), I thought initially that the child would be premature, and would be a Capricorn rather than an Aquarius—especially as the Cancer/Capricorn axis was occurring so frequently. What actually happened was different: she was a Pisces with her Ascendant in the last degrees of Cancer!

Other astrologers with whom I have discussed this have had comparable experiences with their children, so it looks very much as if both parents and the child itself react to something that is going to be expressed in a horoscope that is not yet in existence—that has yet to be born. Clearly, parent and child are already unconsciously aware of it. The question whether the child's horoscope is the result of certain experiences, or is something to which it reacts unconsciously by electing to be born at the moment that suits it best, is something I find unanswerable at present. The fact is that the child makes itself known in accordance with its future radix.

What about children born by induction—does the same thing apply in the presence of outside interference? I know of only one instance where this was so; but that is insufficient evidence for any conclusions to be drawn and, unfortunately, very few professional astrologers take accurate notes of events during pregnancy. All the same, in the charts of children whose birth dates were brought forward by induction or were delivered by Cesarean section, the 12th house is usually quite apt in representing their mythic phase and their sensitivity. The surgical intervention seems hardly to matter. On the other hand, I (and other astrologers) have observed that, in a child whose birth has been induced, the Moon or the Ascendant is less likely to fit the family picture well. But the last word has not been said on this.

In the main, adopted children blend remarkably well into the astrological picture of their new parents, including the 12th-house area. This is especially true of those adopted as babies; but even children adopted at a later stage still show correspondences, although sometimes less perceptibly in the 12th house. Anyway, somehow or other, the child is likely to go where it fits in. Carl Jung's theory of synchronicity presupposes a latent meaning in existence through which we come chiefly into those circumstances that suit our psyches. It is as if we attract them even though at first sight they have the appearance of being accidental. The fact that children's birth charts so often match the astrological profiles of their adoptive parents, is a fair indication that Jung was thinking along the right lines.

Although, in the above, we have confined our attention to the role of parents and adoptive parents, experience teaches that, when a child is entrusted for a long time to the care of a third party, the youngster will react to the unconscious of this person too. Especially when a baby of some six weeks or two months is left at a day care center during the day will the psyche of the attendant exert a big influence on it. Then the situation will almost be like having a surrogate parent; occasional little visits do not count.

To sum up, we can say that a child seems to respond to a horoscope that its actual date and time of birth have yet to decide; probably even when this date and time are going to be chosen by some obstetrician. Adopted children, too, fall into this pattern; and a regular childcare giver can also influence operation of the 12th house.

Additional Questions

In the 12th house, we often find things that play an unconscious role in the parents and also awaken a response in the child. If one of these things is a problem; and in the course of time, the problem becomes consciously recognized and solved—is this a help, or does the child still have to be burdened with the problem? And if the child has hard aspects to the ruler of the 12th, does this reduce the parents' chances of solving the problem? Can such a contingency be read from the horoscope? Can one see the unlived life of the parents moved into the horoscopes of their children? Does one of the parents have the same planet in the 12th or in aspect with the ruler of the 12th? Does the 12th house contain influences other than those of the parents?

As far as the last question is concerned, we have already answered it in previous chapters. So many other factors appear to be involved that it would be quite unjustified to go on a witch-hunt, and we must certainly not blame our parents for what we find in our 12th house. To be more specific, if your child has Pluto in the 12th, that can mean that you or your partner had a Plutonic process going on under the surface, or that a crisis was brewing. Also, I have frequently met this placement where the parents found themselves in very trying circumstanes, e.g., when they were living with in-laws and one of the child's grandparents was so domineering that the parents were in a state of tension. Or one or more deaths had taken place in the family during the pregnancy or around the birth of the child. The theme of life and death is always linked with Pluto. But, in a positive sense, it can also mean that one of the parents possesses a talent ruled by Pluto and is not using it and perhaps is unaware of it. Thus a child with Pluto in the 12th, whose mother took up the study of psychology later in life, is a case in point. It turned out greatly to the mother's advantage when her latent gift was developed.

Venus in the 12th need not imply clandestine love affairs, as the books often tell us. Of course, it is possible that your parents had a difficult relationship if your Venus is in the 12th; but it is equally possible that one of them had artistic talents which were not exploited. Here again I can think of a mother who started painting "just for a joke" when her grown-up daughter did. The daughter had Venus in the 12th, and painting is now the mother's meat and drink. It has completely brightened her life, and what she produces is excellent.

The ways in which horoscope factors work out are so numerous that it is impossible to make a success of them all. Of necessity, there is always something hanging fire in the unconscious. Sometimes it is held back deliberately; often the fault is due to the pressure of everyday living. How many of us have found that during the period when we are hard at work carving out a career for ourselves, we are also looking after a young family? Among other things, this period is one in which certain psychic factors, skills and problems have to be left on one side. Anyway, it is a perfectly normal state of affairs, and there is no need to blame anyone for it. For a parent to entertain feelings of guilt solves nothing, for the child will inevitably pick those feelings up. In any case, guilt feelings can be developed as a sort of "lightning conductor" in order to escape having to face the real problem. I am not saying that we must bear no responsibility for our actions—quite the reverse— but the usual idea of guilt and penance in the Saturnian sense of cause and effect is not very compatible with the collective nature of this house. Whatever may be said about the 12th house of our children, it remains a rich house. If it is viewed as the access to the source of our life (the well of water), we shall see how through our behavior we can help our children find the way to their own inner source. On the other hand, it can lead us back to our own forgotten or unknown dreams, longings and hidden talents.

Years and years ago, I liked making music and enjoyed drawing and writing poetry. But there was so much to do, what with having to work besides raising a family, that nothing ever came of these interests. After all, I thought, one can't do everything, and I put these forms of creativity out of my mind. I still enjoyed listening to music, but completely stopped performing it. It did not seem like a great loss. And then my daughter was born, with her ruler of the 12th conjunct Venus. She has an exceptional musical ear, loves to sing and dance, and merrily leads me back to a world of music I had imagined I no longer needed. She is always begging me to play a tune on the piano for us to sing together, and she likes to dance around with me. And I enjoy it. She has shown me a side of myself that I had neglected too soon, and now I realize what I have been missing! What is more, the connection between Venus and the 12th house follows a family pattern. My maternal grandfather made some superb drawings but never exploited his gift. My mother has the ruler of the 12th in the 2nd house—a placement that often points to (inherited) artistic ability. Now, in later life, she is very active musically and artistically, and makes the most beautiful things. At the time of my birth, however, her talents were still undeveloped. I have the ruler of the 12th square Venus in my chart!

In this respect children can be very positive and valuable. But what if their behavior makes a shrewd point about something irksome one has repressed? Naturally, that is not so pleasant. What happens then depends on how much readiness there is to come to terms with the problem. If a child highlights something of which one is afraid, and one fails to react properly, there is a big chance that the child will share the fear and become adversely affected. A father with Neptune in the 12th who possessed paranormal gifts but was terribly frightened of them, had a child with the same placement of Neptune—a child who could almost read his mind! He has warned the child not to dabble in psychic matters, yet has no idea why it has developed so many anxieties and phobias. This is the less happy side of the placement.

It is impossible to tell from a horoscope whether the mainly constructive or the mainly destructive influence of the 12th house will be developed by the native. The potential for good or ill is all that lies in the house, astrologically speaking. So helping the child through this area is one of the biggest responsibilities of parents. By what they are and do they can teach the child, without too many fears and tensions and stresses, how to handle 12th-house factors. And they can learn a lot about themselves at the same time.

When, in the course of time, irrespective of the child's age, the parents open their eyes to their problems and the consequences of them, and try to solve them, that is sure to influence the child. One way or another, we all remain linked to our parents.

This can sometimes have crucial results, as in the example given by Frances Wickes in her book *The Inner World of Childhood*.[8] A mother came to her in despair. Her son had left her. She had devoted her whole life to him, and done everything for him, and had lived a life that was anything but her own. She was suicidal, but the slight chance that he might return and need her kept her from doing anything rash. She went for analysis, and after a difficult period in which she worked hard on her dreams there came a moment in one of the sessions when she suddenly altered. All at once it dawned on her that she could and should lead her own life. She said, "I am going to pick up the threads of my life and learn to live it, even if I never see him again. My grief will never go away, but it is my own life that I am going to live from now on." It was the end of the session, and the clock struck twelve. Three days later a letter arrived, dated the day of her decision. It read: "Dear Mother, I am sitting here on a hill three thousand miles away from you. I have just heard the clock strike nine, and the fear I have always carried round with me has suddenly lifted. I am returning home." Twelve o'clock in the mother's time zone was the same moment as nine o'clock in the son's time zone.

A child always carries something of its parents. Therefore, generally speaking, it is very helpful to the child when the parents work on themselves. But the child also has its own character, and will make its own decisions one way or another; and, later on, will make up its own mind whether to tackle or shelve certain problems. And so we must not assume that the parents have failed when the child does not seem to be doing too well. Several times I have talked with parents who, in all honesty, have tried to cope with their problems, and have not ceased to struggle with themselves in spite of all the anxiety and uncertainty that this involves. They lamented, "It looks as if our child will have to tackle the root of the problem all over again, just as though nothing in us had really changed." And yet the parents had changed quite a lot.

---

[8]F.G.Wickes, *The Inner World of Childhood*.

Now, as parents, we must not deprive our children of the right to make their own mistakes. They should be allowed to make their own way through life. If the child's problem is closely related to that of the parents, then it does seem that the child will have to tackle it all over again. But the 12th house is covert: we do not see what is going on under the surface. If as a parent you put a problem right, then under the surface you open a door for your child or for anyone else who is vulnerable to the problem at that moment. The results may not be spectacular outwardly, but the seed has been sown from which something will grow.

Even when the parents fail to work on themselves, a child can break free from the problems of the older generation, and has no need to be burdened by them forever. Whether or not the parents do anything constructive about them is not something we can read either from the horoscopes of the parents or from the horoscope of the child. This means that a child with great conflicts around the 12th house can have wonderful parents who keep working on themselves energetically, while a child with harmonious aspects around the 12th house can have parents who are just as nice, but rely on putting on appearances and therefore solve nothing. So hard aspects in a child's chart need not signify that the child or its parents will not do well.

All connections with the 12th house, whether harmonious or inharmonious, have to do with our earliest experiences. The harmonious do not always relate to hidden talents, and the inharmonious certainly do not always relate to parental problems. I have often encountered problem situations with the harmonious aspects, plus all the uncertainty that goes with them. Therefore, in the first place, we must look to see which factors are linked with the 12th house. These planets are experienced as sources of trouble and insecurity, but we can utilize them to create some alternative form of security.

Here is another point. Suppose you wanted to study but were prevented from doing so by circumstances. When you started a family it was no longer possible. Let us say that your ambition had been to become a doctor. There is a chance that one of your children will have Jupiter (or the ruler of the 12th) in the 12th house or in aspect to the ruler of the 12th. However, this does not imply that your child will also have its heart set on becoming a doctor, or that there will be some uncertainty about it. That a parent's psychic situation can activate a pattern in the child, tells us that the pattern (or planet) can manifest itself in other ways too. In the example just given of Jupiter, the child might easily want to be a doctor in a big hospital when it grows up. But he or she might want to travel the globe instead, with a view to studying what can be done about the problems of the third world. One is not confined to exactly the same problem as that faced by one's parents. The possibilities are many, and it is not a question of being forced into one's parents' mold.

Hence the unlived life of the parents or surrogate parents creates all sorts of problems, but at the same time opens up new dimensions of possibilities. Nothing in the horoscope is wholly good or wholly bad. All chart placements possess both sides. This applies equally to trines *and* squares of the ruler of the 12th. If we consider in this light the question of whether or not any development in the unlived life of the parents can be inferred from the horoscopes of the younger children, then we must say that one is unable to see (and must not state) that the parents do better or worse because, for example, the first child had a trine and the second child a square. In that respect, we can conclude nothing. What is revealed in the horoscopes of children, however, is the situation in which they are unconsciously embedded, and how they experience this situation. If a child is born with a strong 12th house then, below the surface in the family, all sorts of changes are going on that could shortly come to the surface. This need not always be accompanied by crises and rows. I have observed that young children with a heavily tenanted 12th house often grow up in problem situations in their early years; sometimes openly, sometimes not. One situation is successfully negotiated, but not another. What we can never do is to predict the outcome of 12th house influences from the child's chart.

The present chapter has given us an opportunity to examine the role of the parents in some depth; in the next chapter we shall place this role in a broader framework.

6

Yin and Yang in General, or Mom and Dad in Particular?

Are Father and Mother Present in the Chart?

In the previous chapter we saw that in the 12th house of the child we can find information about the unlived life of its parents, and about what is going on below the surface in the environment of the newborn baby. This raises the question of whether or not a child's horoscope can provide information about what the parents really made of themselves; a question involving an astrological discussion as to where precisely the parents are located in the chart.

According to classical astrology, the Moon represents the mother and the Sun the father. In addition, Saturn is supposed to have a good deal to do with the father and Venus with the mother. Houses 4 and 10 also play an important role. But whereas one astrologer assigns the father to the 10th and the mother to the 4th, another does the exact opposite (mother to the 10th and father to the 4th), and another again is of the opinion that the more dominant parent belongs to the 10th and the more submissive to the 4th. In other words, astrologers speak with one voice on the tie-up of parents and planets, but do not agree about the houses.

The lack of agreement on the attribution of planets and houses to the two parents is due among other things to the notion that a clearcut partition can be made between them. Of course, there is an obvious difference between male and female: they form a polarity on which the whole of life is based. But, as the Chinese T'ai-chi or Yin-Yang symbol teaches, the white always contains a particle of black and the black a particle of white. In Jungian psychology, every male psyche has a female part and every female psyche a male part. Edward Whitmont, a Jungian analyst, remarks on this point that male and female characteristics, hormones, organs, archetypal tendencies, complexes and character traits, are inseparably linked to the life-functions of both sexes. Whether someone is a man or a woman depends on a relative preponderance of one sex over another. The prevailing sex stamps itself on the conscious mind, the elementary psychic structure, and the physical appearance. The characteristics of the other sex are suppressed and function more as an unconscious potential. Jung named the feminine potential in the unconscious of the man his anima, and the masculine potential in the unconscious of the woman her animus.

Without going too deeply into the question of the animus and the anima, it is important to note that Jungian psychology attaches a great deal of importance to the man coming into contact with his anima or unconscious feminine side, and accepting it and giving it a place, and to the woman doing the same with her animus. Animus and anima behave differently in the two sexes, but that need not worry us here. What should concern us is properly coming to terms with the "other sex" in our psyches; or, in Chinese symbolism, not blanking out the black dot in the white field, but learning to value and integrate it. The symbolism actually represents this integration.

It is vital to be able to recognize, respect and integrate our unconscious side, because it plays such a significant part in our relationships and contacts with the outside world. When a man does not understand and respect his inner feminine side, or even denies it, he will leave this side of himself undeveloped. It is a side that is also often projected, so there is a danger that he will project an immature image on feminine persons, that he will have false hopes of them, that his attitude toward them will be maladjusted, and his reactions unbalanced. This can involve all his contacts with women, including mother, sister, wife, doctor, school-mistress, secretary, etc. But even his contacts with men can be affected; though more through the creation of unpleasant atmospheres where all sorts of heavily disguised feelings can spoil relationships. But, whatever the case, as long as there is no relative balance between male and female on the inside, there will be no balance on the outside. Or, to state the general rule, we always seemingly become drawn into circumstances (or, would it be more accurate to say that we unconsciously maneuver ourselves into circumstances?) that reflect the total state of our psyches.

This means that a man with an undeveloped anima is likely to fall in love with a woman who is similarly lacking in inner balance. Therefore all sorts of unconscious factors can upset their relationship at the most unpredictable moments. Of course, the same is true for a woman, although her animus expresses itself differently from the anima. The failure to develop her animus, her inner male potential, can impede her way of functioning too, as Emma Jung demonstrated so well in her book *Animus and Anima*[9]; also Sanford in *The Invisible Partner*[10] illustrated the same thing rather beautifully.

In forming an astrological theory, it is important to stop and think at this point; what exactly does a child experience with the Sun in the 12th house? Is it something to do with the father, or can the unconscious masculine side of the mother come into the picture? Is the Moon solely the representative of the mother, or can it also say something about the unconscious female side of the father? Or does it have a wider application? In other words, does the Moon tell us about everything to do with the female principle as such, and so embrace the whole feminine part of the family, and not just the mother? Or has the Moon nothing to say about the sphere outside the child, but only something about the innate reaction of the child to the mother and to what is feminine, without any real reference to the external situation? I shall attempt to answer these questions in the following paragraphs on the basis of what I have found in practice.

One last point on the connection between the parents and the houses. Even though the mother (simply in an archetypal role, if you like) plays a very important part, a newborn infant seems, for

---

[9]Emma Jung, *Animus and Anima* (Dallas: Spring Publications, 1983).
[10]J.A. Sanford, *The Invisible Partner* (Mahwah, NJ: Paulist Press, 1980).

many months, to make no distinction between the mother and the father (or whoever is looking after it, male or female). This can be proved by the following example: when a baby of a few months is being held by one of the parents (or regular attendants) and the other parent leaves the room, it does not react to the departure even though it sees what has happened. In a child of one and a half, the result is completely different. It may protest loudly when one parent goes away, even though the other parent remains and it feels completely safe. At this age, there is a much greater appreciation of different persons each with their own meaning. So, originally, there is an experience of unity, which does not become differentiated until later, in the sense that the single unit of the family is seen to be composed of separate personalities. In my opinion, the original undivided unity experienced by the child justifies the belief that the two parents share houses 4 and 10—in other words, we should not say that one house belongs to one parent and the other house to the other parent.

Jung's vision also points in this direction. If it is true that the opposite sex is psychologically active in each sex (both outwardly and inwardly), then, obviously, it becomes more difficult to make hard and fast distinctions; especially as it is indisputable that men and women influence each other in all kinds of ways. A fairly graphic example is that of the woman who projects her driving force on her husband, sets him hard at work for her, gives him targets to achieve and urges him to seek promotion or anything else she has in mind, so that she can bask in the glory of his importance. It is hard to say, in such a case, which of the parents is more dominant (and, according to some, must be placed in the 10th house). Even the case of the pitifully dependent husband whose ill-health or feeble nature leaves him under the control of a strong wife who decides everything that happens to him, is not as straightforward as it seems. His physical or mental disability may also give him the opportunity to play on his partner unconsciously and put her in a position she can not avoid. Under the surface there may be very great domination. So which of them is really the stronger? Who belongs to the 10th house and who to the 4th? It is my experience that sometimes the mother fits better into the 10th house, and sometimes the father does, but usually each of them belongs to both houses.

Following these short theoretical illustrations, I shall run through a number of examples from my own case book. Sections 2, 3 and 4 deal with the father/mother theme in connection with the 12th house and the Sun, Moon, and Saturn, and will state some of my conclusions. Sections 6 and 7 will also deal with the Sun, Moon and Saturn, but within a wider framework. The emphasis will be laid on practical experience.

Sun in the 12th House

It has repeatedly seemed to me that, with these aspects, young children have had fathers who have played no more than a minor role in their lives, especially during all or most of their early years. The causes are multifarious, although seldom suggesting a lack of good intentions on the part of the parents. Many of these causes have come to light during consultations and workshops on the 12th house. Thus, the father may have died just before the birth or during the first few years of the child's life; or the parents may have separated during this period. In either event, the child not only misses the father's influence but, through the symbiotic link with the mother, probably shares in her experience of the problems of the situation; in particular, her efforts to cope with the loss of her husband through death or divorce. The child experiences the problem caused by the male.

On the other hand, a child with the Sun in the 12th can have a father who comes home every day as regular as clockwork and appears to do his duty by his family. And yet, when we look into the matter, we find in a number of cases that the father is not really interested in his children or feels that they are depriving him too much of his wife's attention. Sometimes the father is always doing odd jobs about the house, or sitting in his study, or lounges around drinking, or has little to contribute. And here we come to the role of the mother; for the Sun in the 12th can also indicate a very dominant mother who elbows the father out of the way and does not let him near the children, or thinks of the children as her exclusive possessions and separates them psychologically from the father.

And there are further possibilities. For example, there are the children who are born when the parents are struggling to establish themselves financially—perhaps they have their own business, and the father has to work all the time. I myself have spoken with the fathers of children with the Sun in the 12th who are quite aware of what they are doing and say something like this: "In the first years of life, the child needs the mother much more than the father. If I work hard now, I shall have more time to spend with the children later on when they are a bit older and need me more." Very fine-sounding sentiments, no doubt, however, the fact remains that, with the Sun in the 12th, the child does need something paternal in its surroundings, even though the parent concerned may not see this clearly.

On the other hand, I have encountered situations in which the placement of the Sun in the 12th house looks rather odd, because both parents did a lot for their children and were genuinely happy with them and with each other. Quite often it has transpired that, around the time the child was born, one of these parents was having a problem with his or her own father; either going through an internal struggle over him or actively quarreling with him. Or one of the parents may have passed through a more or less serious identity crisis at that time.

Also what may happen is that, during the first few years of the child's life, the father is in the hospital or in a sanatorium; in other words he is away from home for health reasons. Alternatively, it may be the child who has been hospitalized early in life and has felt its security threatened for a shorter or longer period.

Many different cases could be quoted where some problem is involved. But a problem is certainly not involved in every case; and where none exists it seems that the prominence of the 12th house is due simply to a strong Piscean influence inherited from one or both parents—say from a father with the Sun, Ascendant or Moon in Pisces. And I have also met the Sun in the 12th house of children whose mother had a Pisces Sun, Moon or Ascendant, even though the Sun is naturally more representative of the father.

At this point, I want to emphasize what I said before, which is that in most instances neither parent is to blame when a child with the Sun in the 12th is caught up in a difficult situation such as admittance to hospital, or when the child inherits less desirable family character traits, or when it is born at a time when one or both of the parents are undergoing far-reaching psychic development. In any case, if the development is allowed to take its course, this can turn out very profitably for the child. And although cases of neglect occur in which the parents do deserve to be blamed, we should never jump to conclusions about the 12th-house sun position.

These few examples demonstrate that although it is possible to say something about the child's first years (and perhaps about its prenatal life), it is impossible to tell from the chart alone precisely what has taken place. Even less does the person of the father himself always come into the picture with the Sun in the 12th or aspecting the ruler of the 12th. The mother may be the important one. Also some fear or anxiety may be involved, such as is felt by a young child who is taken to hospital. The Sun here is more general in its symbolism than would be the case if it was simply a pointer to the father.

Saturn in the 12th *(Chuck)* *(Patricia ∞)*

It is remarkable how often we find Saturn in the 12th or in aspect *(me)* to the ruler of the 12th in the charts of children whose fathers were absent or hardly ever present in their early youth. The result is therefore very like that of the Sun in the 12th. But there are in fact differences. Here are some examples: in some instances, one of the parents seems to have no initiative, perhaps through a lack of backbone, and relies very heavily on the other, or puts on a hard front to disguise the weakness and avoid facing up to it. The baby picks the problem up via the psychic umbilical chord. In other cases both parents have a problem: one of them leans on the other and draws strength from him or her, while the other gains an identity as a helpmate—but this is only a cloak to cover a sense of inadequacy. In practice, the sex of the parent does not matter a jot: both have to do with Saturn in the 12th house.

The difference from the Sun in the 12th is that the Sun is much involved with identity problems, with the feeling of being oneself; whereas Saturn in the 12th or in aspect to the ruler of the 12th has more to do with inner backbone, with the finding of a certain measure of stability in life and in the form or structure one gives one's life, and with the structure within which one is free to be oneself.

Just as with the Sun in the 12th, with Saturn here we encounter parents who had problems with their own parents or, at least, were trying to come to terms with the parents, and this affects the child. This also occurs with the Moon in the 12th, but much less frequently. Also a repressed feeling of loneliness, or a feeling of loneliness held at bay, in one of the parents (or similarly repressed inferiority feelings), can go with Saturn in the 12th or in aspect to the ruler of the 12th. In conversations with parents of children with Saturn in the 12th, I have sometimes heard the mothers say that they found their life situations completely unsatisfactory. These mothers were usually those nowadays called "surburban widows," living in a quiet, unexciting part of town, far away from where their husbands' work. Every morning the men leave home before the crack of dawn and do not get back until late in the evening. The children are at school all day, and the mothers do not feel settled in the environment where they live and work. Some of them reach for the sherry bottle before eleven o'clock in the morning for solace.

Sometimes Saturn in the 12th or aspecting the ruler of the 12th expresses itself in inherited characteristics. One child had a crooked back, and the parents had suffered with back problems from an early age. Another example is that of a child with deformed feet—a problem that went back in the family to one of the grandfathers. More often, I have not seen physical problems, although I have regularly heard of people with Saturn in the 12th or in aspect to the ruler of the 12th who suffered from cold feet and/or backaches. In fact there seems to be some connection here.

Again, with Saturn in connection to the 12th house, we see a great number of problem situations. But there may be exceptions. I once talked with an astrologer who had Saturn in the 12th, who belonged to a large family where all the children have Saturn in the 12th. She could think of no problems associated with the placement and was perfectly satisfied with her situation. Although it is wise to treat with care the evidence of the conscious mind concerning what are usually unconscious processes, I regard the case important enough to mention. There is a not altogether impossible chance that, during the many years in which all the children were passing through their mythic phase, the parents were facing one persistent problem. Perhaps something was inherited from the parents that the parents did not see as a problem, because it was unconsciously integrated into their characters. Thus although a rather difficult situation is often found, this is not a hard and fast rule.

Moon in the 12th House

Whatever applies to the Sun in the 12th house, more or less applies to the Moon in the 12th. However, the Moon in the 12th or in aspect to the ruler of the 12th more often relates to the mother's situation, and the Sun in the 12th more often to the father's situation. I often encounter the Moon in the 12th or aspecting the ruler of the 12th in cases where the child has experienced too little maternal care during all or part of the first few years of life. And I regularly see this placement in premature babies, who are treated very clinically, and are obliged to miss a great deal of love and attention and psychic bonding in the first days or weeks of life. For all the technical perfection of an incubator, and for all the skill of the nursing staff who look after the physical well-being of the infant, these are no substitutes for the warmth, tenderness and closeness of the mother. Obviously, this vital lack is intensely felt by children with the Moon in the 12th or in aspect to the ruler of the 12th. As far as I can make out, the duration of the incubator period does not matter so much as the amount of distress experienced. Even children who for other reasons have to spend some time in hospital in these first years, can have this fact reflected by the Moon (or Sun) in the 12th or in aspect to the ruler of the 12th. The Moon tends to represent the shock of being thrust into a new and dangerous situation.

I have seen the same connection between the Moon and the 12th house where the mother lay in hospital for a certain time, or ran away from home, or suffered from post-natal depression; in short, in situations where the child had to do without the intimate contact with its mother, or the mother was unable to show her feelings to the child.

Another possibility is that, in the first years of the child's life, one of the parents is wrestling (internally or externally) with the relationship to his or her own mother. Also, in consequence of the pregnancy and birth, the child's mother may suddenly experience a problem with her femininity. This can be quite a separate issue from wanting a child. Some women are upset that they have to spend a longish period looking fat and out of shape. Women who have always associated their femininity with a slim figure and ideal vital statistics, can have enormous difficulties in adjusting to their new look. For the child, this can be represented by a link between the Moon and the 12th house. But even women who do not suffer from this problem or do so only to a slight extent, can go through a period when, for example, they feel differently about themselves or come to the conclusion that they are different from what they thought they were. In short there is a certain amount of unrest over the feminine identity of the mother.

In other cases, the Moon in the 12th or aspecting the ruler of the 12th in a child's chart indicated a weak or emotionally troubled or very exacting mother; and sometimes, according to my informants, it was the father who was moody and immature. Once again, it is difficult to say which parent will be involved, even if one (in this instance the mother) is the more likely candidate. Occasionally, the home atmosphere seems to be inexplicably unsettled, or else the family is simply too big for the children to be given much individual attention, and the child in question is brought up more by its older sisters and brothers than by its parents. Once or twice I have seen that, in the native's first few years of life, the mother or a little sister died; but this is exceptional.

Of course, I have come across connections between the Moon and the 12th house in which there were no problems in the above sense. In the cases I have investigated, one or both parents were very sensitive, paranormally gifted, or possessed an active social conscience, etc. In the charts of these parents, Pisces or the 12th house was often tenanted, or the planet Neptune was prominent (e.g., on the MC in one parent's chart and conjunct the Sun in the other's!). This can be splendid for family life, showing lots of love and no problems. We have to remember, however, that not every child with such a position will follow the good example. After things have gone well for so long that harmony is taken for granted, people tend to stop working on their relationships and problems start to rear their heads again in the next generation. This is in perfect accord with the law that everything turns into its opposite, the law that Jung called *enantiodromia*. Thus one can grow up well balanced with nothing to worry about and then pass through certain trials that are shadows of the successful run of things, until a middle path is consciously found.

Some Conclusions

As we review the foregoing, several points catch the eye. First, the Sun, Moon and Saturn (and naturally the other planets, too) can refer either to the father or to the mother. Secondly, planets in the 12th or aspecting the ruler of the 12th, very often indicate problem situations in keeping with their nature. Thirdly, given the variety of possible outcomes and relationships, one can not apportion blame. Fourthly, it seems that the 12th house also reflects a certain inherited sensitivity—again from one or both parents. Lastly, because no clear line of demarcation can be drawn between father and mother; and because the 12th house represents a sphere that is not restricted to the parents, we have to be very careful how we interpret it. This brings us to the question of how far the sensitivity of the child itself is a deciding factor in the situation. For one thing not all premature babies without a link between the Moon and the 12th house are hugged and given constant attention by their parents! The way premature babies experience things must vary.

Consider the following. I once cast horoscopes for a twin brother and sister. Not more than 30 minutes separated their times of birth, but the gap was sufficient for several marked differences to appear in the charts. It was striking that the brother had Pluto in the 12th house, whereas the sister, who was born first, had Pluto in the 1st house. The brother was always more sensitive to the father's grim anxiety, which the latter tried to hide by behaving in a Plutonic manner in society. The father rose to the top, while the son withdrew into his shell and, so to speak, exhibited to the world his father's actual fear of life. The sister, with Pluto in the 1st, was quite different. She was less influenced by this side of her father's character, and was quite belligerent and self-reliant. She frequently took her brother's part and challenged her father's authority by doing so.

Here, then, we have two children, born at practically the same time, but with a different 12th house. Their behavior seems to show that the 12th house says something not only about the situation and attitude of the parents, but more especially about the child's innate sensitivity to certain facets of these. Which brings us back to our original question of whether the chicken or the egg came first, a question that was amply discussed in the previous chapter. But, in concluding the present chapter, let us take a further look at the backgrounds and modes of influence of the Sun, Moon and Saturn in the 12th or in aspect to the ruler of the 12th.

The Sun Again

The Sun in the 12th or aspecting the ruler of the 12th is still regarded in some quarters as prejudicial, troublesome and even downright evil. The danger is that the powerful opportunities offered by such a position will be overlooked, and that fear of its bad side will produce a self-fulfilling vicious spiral. By this I mean that the individual thinks that he or she is ignorant and inadequate, beset by every imaginable evil power, and "incapable of achieving anything." Day after day, this person feeds his or her mind with a negative hypnotic suggestion which is not long in coming true. Nevertheless, this does not prove that such a position of the Sun always signifies all this misery.

The truth of the matter is that a part of what the child uses to form its identity is taken from the father (or from the male or yang aspect of the environment into which it is born), and this is not without its problems. These problems can continue far into adult life. The child experiences identity problems and does not know their origin. In one way or another, processes the child cannot understand hinder it from forming an identity. A child with the Sun in the 12th or aspecting the ruler of the 12th needs a great deal of reassurance from its father—usually much more than is given, or can be given. Sometimes the father figure is absent; yet sometimes the child gets plenty of attention from both father and mother. In the latter case, one of the parents may be occupied with an assimilation process or with forming their own identity; alternatively, they may have simply pushed their identity to one side.

In this respect, the 12th house is bottomless: however much attention the child receives, it is always aware of a certain inner uncertainty that makes it crave even more attention.

One of the factors the child cannot come to grips with is the high degree of sensitivity. This in itself is a source of great uncertainty. As with any of the planets in the 12th or aspecting the ruler of the 12th, there is a feeling of not really being able to hold on. It is as if such a planet, in this case the Sun, were hidden behind a screen, or dimmed by a mist. These individuals have a loose idea of their whereabouts, but no more than that; and do not know what they will, or can, do with it. With such a Sun, they have doubts about self and about personal identity. They think they do not know what they want even when setting a fixed course to all appearances, and they wonder what sort of life they ought to lead.

On the other hand, there is a lot of energy tucked away in planets in the 12th or in aspect to the ruler of the 12th, waiting for these natives to find out what they can and will do. What is not realized is that with the Sun in this placement, these individuals can be forceful and demanding, and very self-absorbed, without considering that this is at the expense of others. Because they always feel that they are seeking and unsettled, they do not see the threat they pose to others. Yet, to their amazement, they keep leaving others behind them on their way to the top. Even so, their doubts remain, including the doubt as to whether they are on the right track.

Nevertheless, this same Sun in the 12th or aspecting the ruler of the 12th makes these natives better bosses than many others, provided they venture to use the gifts of the 12th house. Their sensitivity is greater than average, especially in regard to appreciation of situations and empathy with employees. A boss like this (regardless of the element to which they belong) who relies on sensitivity without reasoning everything out, will, for example, step out of the office at the right moment to have a quick word with someone on the factory floor, apparently for no particular reason. It later transpires that, at that very moment, the worker had hit a snag and was thinking of taking sick leave for a few days in order to give someone else time to sort it out. The timely intervention of the boss, the friendly chat and warm show of interest, made this unnecessary. Result: fewer sick days and a better work atmosphere.

This natural intuition can also give a feeling for things that are going to become important in future, even though they are still shrouded in mist. Without realizing it, and without knowing why, 12th house people can follow a trend that will yield rich dividends at some future date. They appear to sense the way things are going to go.

Problems arise when these people deny their feelings and intuitive insights. They remain unsure and seek an identity, but do not know how to find a flexible form for it. Consequently, they tend to have too much to say for themselves and can run into all kinds of problems with those around them, with colleagues, friends, the family and so on. These problems arise out of excessive preoccupation with self, and out of a readiness to take offense because the tenuous feeling of security is so easily threatened. Being rather disoriented, they are unable to follow the lead of their feelings. Often there is either hardness out of anxiety, or an exaggerated subservience—a form of self-sacrifice that almost says: "Accept my help or be shot!"

One possible result with one or other of the planets in contact with the 12th house is this sort of intrusion with offers of help. It is as if these people use their ability to help to prove themselves, or to provide themselves with a certain identity. To be more precise: by pushing help on someone, they have a good chance of influencing others, of placing others under an obligation or making others dependent, all of which are ego-boosters. It is not easy for the recipients of these attentions to say what is going on, but enough is insinuated in little ways for them to guess what lies below the surface. This is sometimes called underhanded, but wrongly so. For the 12th house people to see through their own behavior is hard if, from early childhood, they have had to contend with double-dealing (e.g., when the words of those who looked after them were belied by what they did), or who lack self-confidence because of their situation or because of parental unreliability. It may take them years to recover from this bad start, but it is possible for them to make a genuine change.

Once these people begin to understand their sensitivity, they can take the first step, which is to accept it. Dreams, so-called unproductive sitting and fantasizing, the realm of symbolism and inner imagery, the effects of music and art and so on, can then be used at an inner level. If they are bold enough to open up to it, intuition and sensitivity will point out the way that is right for them. With such a placement, these people are very close to the source of life, and are able to draw from it; they just need to know how. They are unusually capable of tuning in to an as yet untapped world of energies.

People who interest themselves in homeopathy, acupuncture, reflexology, dream therapy, art therapy, hypnosis, yoga or meditation, and also the tranquilizing property of water, often seem to have a strongly emphasized 12th house, and frequently a link between the Moon and the 12th.

The line of demarcation between dream and reality is less clear in the 12th house than it is in other houses. It is as if the archetypal ideas that dwell in us all more easily come to the surface here. Inner archetypal images place an enormous force at our disposal; this can be seen by the way they inspire artists, scientists and others (see chapter 8, "The creative power of the unconscious"). But life can also be weakened by these images because they may overwhelm us with ideas and emotions that may not all be useful. The inner life is effervescent and, admittedly, may subtly lead us in accordance with our nature; but sometimes, when we live too close to the source of the images, we find that one of them latches on to some complex or other and becomes obsessive. We are taken over by an idea and the ego becomes inflated: we believe we are special, often because we serve a so-called impersonal ideal. Or we have a guru-complex, or a desire to save the world—perhaps as a self-appointed messiah.

These are the hidden dangers.

Those who are a match for 12th-house energies, who dare to take a steady look at themselves and are prepared to work on themselves, will observe a kind of wisdom flowing through them—hard to pin down perhaps, but always there when needed. This wisdom is available for all areas of life, not just for those who have the Sun in the 12th or in aspect to the ruler of the 12th. One of the keynotes is to dare to tackle our sensitivity, vulnerability and impressionability, to accept the world of the illogical and symbolic, to acknowledge the reality of the unconscious, and enhance our everyday reality.

The Moon and a Little Bit of Saturn . . .

Just as the Sun very broadly represents the paternal and masculine, so the Moon broadly represents the maternal and feminine. A child with the Moon in the 12th or in aspect to the ruler of the 12th craves security. As with the Sun in the 12th or in aspect to the ruler of the 12th, the emotional life is very rich, and there is great empathy and intuition. Fantasy is well-developed, and sensitivity and reaction to the environment is much greater than in the average person.

Others' feelings are picked up quickly and, with such a placement, it can be initially hard to tell their feelings apart from ours. We are easily affected by stirring events, and scenes of suffering make a particularly powerful impression. Often this creates a desire to support groups in need of protection for some reason. It makes no difference whether we find an outlet in the protection of animals, in aid for Amnesty International, or in helping the third world, junkies, alcoholics, orphans or threatened rain forests. We may even start a refuge for injured hedgehogs hit by cars, so that they can be healed and returned to the wild. What matters (even if we are male) is to be able to lavish our care and maternal feelings on vulnerable people, animals and groups with one thing in common: their world is at a certain distance from our own.

Although so emotionally involved, we avoid expressing our feelings on a person-to-person basis. To do so would make us uneasy and uncomfortable. Just as people with the Sun in the 12th have problems with general manifestation and displaying the individuality, so those with a link between the Moon and the 12th house have the same trouble with displaying feelings—especially where hugging and kissing are concerned. I have frequently heard people with Moon in the 12th or in aspect to the ruler of the 12th say something like this: ". . . then I sat down beside so-and-so, and he poured out his heart to me. I felt real sorry for him, but I could not bring myself to put my arm round him and comfort him. That never works for me I guess. I sure would have liked to, but . . . ." There is the problem in a nutshell. Although there is an enormous need to give and receive intimacy and warmth when the Moon is in 12, or aspecting the ruler of 12, fear or incapacity is felt when these are expected, and these people either freeze or clam up.

Because people with such a placement can be rather calculating in what they do, they may deliberately go where it is possible to care for others at arm's length. They are quite likely to accept unpaid or temporary work they know they can quit in a few months: they also take jobs where there is no need or opportunity to throw a friendly arm round someone.

This does not mean that there is no possibility of improvement! But it does take time to build up the necessary inner self-confidence. The Moon in the 12th or aspecting the ruler of the 12th frequently goes with a feeling of lack of success—possibly because of the absence of security in early youth. This feeling lurks under the surface in various spheres of life. Thus it can manifest itself as a sense of worthlessness, a feeling that life is not worth living, and maybe an inferiority complex. These people find that they are not paid for their services because they failed to set a price on them. Or they find that they are unable to have children because they are not "up to it." Sometimes this negative attitude results in sublimation. Thus women who shrink from having children may work in child welfare! They may help in a kindergarten, or perhaps in an animal refuge or zoo. Women with this placement can have difficulties with self-image. They may wonder whether they would ever be good mothers, or have doubts over what it means to be a woman, over what motherhood entails, and so on. Sometimes the scales are tipped on the other side, so that they have a highly exaggerated identification with whatever is feminine, even to the point of obsession. Thus some women with Moon in the 12th, or aspecting the ruler of the 12th can passionately identify with a certain female in mythology, or take up the torch of feminism. In many cases, these powerful (emotional) reactions finally lead to a better understanding of what is going on internally, and to a degree of balance.

In men the effects are somewhat different. Often I see men searching for a sort of mother-goddess in the hope that she will bestow bliss, heaven on earth—and the usual tender embraces. The danger is that they will project the need for a goddess on women in general and on their own wives in particular, so that the women become fictional characters whom they never get to know. There is a similarity here to Venus in the 12th or aspecting the ruler of the 12th, but with this difference—that (so to speak) the man with a lunar influence wants to be wrapped and cherished in the mantle of his semi-divine woman, whereas the man with a Venusian influence wants to put her on a pedestal.

There is no need for men with a link between the Moon and the 12th house to feel too upset when they find that their goddess wears the pants in their relationship and that they have ended up under her authority and control. Once they realize that it happened because they were so open that they allowed their women to rule their emotions, they can handle it. More positively is the strong emotional bond with the partner, a bond that may even be telepathic.

The Moon in the 12th, or in aspect to the ruler of the 12th, makes people very vulnerable emotionally. If they have no insight into this, there is a danger that they will think they are governing their emotions; instead, they have merely buried them for fear of what might be revealed. In such cases, we quite often observe emotional manipulation: moods and atmospheres are simulated in an attempt to control the environment surreptitiously. Clinging to others in order to control emotionally is another possibility. This controlling, however, is really a cry of distress: "Please give me emotional support!" People who fall into this sort of behavior are usually so off-balance emotionally that they do not see any harm in what they are doing. All sorts of incomprehensible processes can then disturb the atmosphere. And yet people with the Moon in the 12th have a lot of friendship, warmth and love to offer. When they feel at ease, and have learned to handle their vulnerability and insecurity, they can display a real interest in others, and a deep insight into symbolism. They can be self-sacrificing without being completely self-effacing; and others feel secure with these individuals who once felt so insecure.

As I have already discussed, the Moon in the 12th (or in aspect to the ruler of the 12th) can have profound consequences for a relationship, especially for a marriage or for a couple living together. The Sun in this position has the same effect. Paradoxically, the native looks for a strong partner while being inclined to play the role of the strong partner too. But, in my experience, Saturn in the 12th or in aspect to the ruler of the 12th has an even greater influence on the relationship with the life partner. We have all read that, with Saturn in the 7th house, the native is likely to seek an older partner; but, as I have said earlier, I have seen this more often with Saturn in the 12th or in the 8th. Perhaps the reason is that, with Saturn in the 12th or in aspect to the ruler of the 12th, the individual is looking for backbone. This person wants a partner who will hold his or her hand through life. Ideally, the partner would be someone of the same age who would help; but in most cases, the desire for a nursemaid as a partner induces the person to turn to a father or mother figure. With the Sun or Moon, the need for firm support and backbone is not so acute, but Saturn represents learning through pain. It is that force within that propels this individual into learning situations. And so, in looking for someone to supply strength, he or she can fall in love with an overpowering mother or father figure who runs their life regardless of any say he or she might like to have in it; and it is only after inner flight (and perhaps divorce) that this person starts to realize what is wrong. Alternatively, this type may be attracted to someone who looks very strong but is the complete opposite (which also happens with Sun/12th-house connections). Then this person is forced to make decisions for the chosen partner and is then obliged to develop the necessary backbone and grit. Another way out can be marriage with an invalid partner, in the (unconscious) knowledge that there will be no need to take responsibility for an intimate relationship.

Here is an example from one of many student reports on 12th-house experiences. "My mother has Saturn, Mercury, the Sun and Jupiter in the 12th, and has the ruler of the 12th square the Moon." The writer adds, "What specially interests me is how far Saturn and the Sun *must* say something about an 'absent' father, for my mother dotes on her own father and I remember him as the dearest granddad anyone could wish for. Besides my mother's family is noted for being closely knit and sociable. One thing is clear though; in my father she met someone who is childish."

In the present chapter we have already more or less answered the first part of her question. There is no necessity for the 12th house to say anything about the grandfather. Unfortunately nothing is known about any identity problems that may have arisen, or about other matters to do with the 12th house of the student's mother. It is perfectly possible that, with this tenancy of the 12th house, she was prone to idealize certain people. But it is striking that in spite of all her good experiences, Saturn—as the learning process through pain—unconsciously guided her to select a childish partner. This is her share both in the family process and in her own process of individuation.

Finally, I must refer again to Hetty Heyster's words, quoted at the beginning of chapter 5, but repeated here for the sake of convenience: "I was born during the Second World War. When my mother was carrying me she suffered from panic fears whenever there was a bombing raid. When she heard the approach of enemy aircraft, she became completely hysterical. I have a conjunction of the Moon and Pluto in my 12th house, and the Moon is also ruler of the 12th. I myself am over-sensitive to sound. It makes me nervous, and I get very uptight if others are noisy. If the neighbors are playing loud music, I become obsessed, and it can drive me to distraction."

In 1986, transiting Pluto and Neptune made aspects to her radical Moon/Pluto conjunction, and a lot came out into the open. She writes: "There has never been a year in which I have put so much effort into my work, have carried out so many commissions, and have not had a single day's rest apart from the times I was brought low by sheer exhaustion! The aggravation I suffered from noise was often acute; and crashing and banging seemed to be going on everywhere, as on the day when nine policemen raided the house next door after being summoned by the social service of the housing association, and so on."

The theme of a dislike of noise that was, so to speak, imprinted on her during her stay in the womb, came to a head in the year when her Moon/Pluto conjunction in the 12th (and the Moon is ruler of the 12th) received a square from Pluto and an inconjunct from Neptune! At the same time, we see here the exhaustion and low spirits that can be associated with Neptune and Pluto as well as with the 12th house. But that was not all that happened that year. She continues, "That was the year when I conceived the idea of traveling to see the excavations at Çatal Hüyük in central eastern Turkey, the cradle of neolithic civilization and of the cult of the great mother goddess (a culture I rather idolize). I went on to make the crazy and tiring pilgrimage in two weeks. For two days I rode in a rented car through the Taurus mountains to reach this place in central Anatolia, where I met a little old man who guarded the area—and there was absolutely nothing to see, apart from some traces of the dig, which had been discontinued three years previously for lack of proper funding. Although I had been warned about this in the archeological museum in Ankara, I was still disappointed. I had expected to see some depictions of bull's horns at the very least! Fortunately, the old man could speak some English which he had picked up from the archeologists and, rather haltingly, he gave me an account of what he knew. Everything about the journey had a Neptunian tint. In the museum where the finds were preserved, I was fascinated by the clumsy figurines of mother goddesses and stylized bronze bulls with fertility symbols, which gave me the feeling that 'time' has no 'length.' I once had a similiar experience on a trip to the cave drawings in the south of France and north of Spain. The contact made with these pictures of animals gave me a sense of there being 'no distance through time.' The theme of the wild ox and its mate was intensely gripping to me at the time, and has always retained my interest."

With a Moon/Pluto conjunction in the 12th house we have themes such as caves, prehistory, the wild ox (Pluto) and wild cow (the Moon), great mother-goddesses, and the like. In Hetty's experiences, we see how compulsive the 12th house can be: she simply had to go to Catal Hüyük. Although the place itself was a disappointment, the journey released much more in herself than she was able to describe, as she later confessed. Above all, through contact with the primitive themes of mother-goddesses, and caves with prehistoric drawings, she had an almost religious experience of timelessness. In one way or another she had approached an intangible source. But she had made her experience of it tangible. She is a sculptress, and understands as no one else how to capture the essential being of an animal with her art, especially when sculpturing the ancient wild ox. And so she has found her vocation in the terrain of the 12th house, fed by the emotions and experiences of her 12th house Moon/Pluto conjunction. Her work, which may be admired in various zoological gardens, is highly esteemed.

Although we now have a better idea of ways in which the 12th house influence can make itself felt, I am well aware that some of its forms of expression present problems and that the area is never an easy one. In my opinion, this has a lot to do with social attitudes. In our culture, processes and experiences that have to do with the

12th house are never or hardly ever understood. A learning process that involves waiting, so-called unproductivity, uncertainty and the nightside of our existence is completely out of favor. In the following chapter, I shall be discussing the far-reaching consequences this attitude has for our opinion of the 12th house, and the way in which it can hinder us from seeing its enriching side. After this, we shall be able to explore the 12th house as a creative instrument.

7

A
Misunderstood
House

In older astrology books especially, the picture painted of the 12th house is not exactly engaging. Thus, we read such things as, "It is a dark, clandestine and mysterious house." Or, "The activities of the 12th house inevitably involve sacrifice of oneself." "This is the house of serious illnesses, of hospitals, sanatoria, asylums and even prisons." "It's usual name is the house of misery and self-undoing." In other words, most of life's sorrows originate in the 12th house.

We all contact the unconscious quite early on, but the contact is not properly valued by everyone. In itself this could denote the liquidation of personality or the overwhelming of personality. Luckily, some astrologers see the source of inspiration and intuition in the 12th, giving a more positive slant to it. Nevertheless, in the older astrology, the 12th house indicated the sphere of menace, flight, loss, misery, self-destruction, imprisonment, deception, and so on. In a more positive sense, it represented the sea and fishing, religion and monasteries or convents and, according to some, art and music.

Now a set of key-words can in no way describe a house. The sole purpose of mentioning the above concepts, as far as I am concerned, is to provide a thumbnail sketch of what the earlier astrologers taught about the 12th house. It would have been pref-

erable to give the original texts, but as pure illustrations they would
have taken up too much space. What comes across in these texts
is not only the choice of words, but more significantly the tone and
purport of the descriptions. Often more is suggested than is openly
expressed, and many people have been given the idea that the 12th
house is a pitfall that can suddenly swallow us into a state of misery.
This may sound rather excessive; but anyone who has listened year
after year to anxious inquiries about the 12th house from students
who have been doing a bit of self-tuition, will know that something
is amiss. The familiar negative presentation creates fear.

Thus the traditional key-words are not particularly sweet-
sounding, and they drive us to happier topics than such things as
fraud and imprisonment. But what about our willingness to face
astrological problems honestly? Where practitioners of various
kinds have all repeatedly emphasized the gloomy side of the 12th
house in their writings, are we to suppose that there was no basis
in experience for what they wrote? I have no wish to scorn the
astrology of past decades, but I am compelled to observe that it
did tend to paint everything in black and white in a way avoided
by the more psychological astrology of the present day. There were
one or two astrologers who could see some of the nuances, but the
general outlook was fatalistic, and the view of the 12th house was
especially dark and fearful. So, how real was the reality they saw?
Or, to be more explicit, is there anything in our culture that has
contributed to this very negative side of our horoscopes; or is the
negative side *objectively* negative?

The question of the genuineness of the picture of the 12th
house that, until a short time ago, has been painted in astrology,
is one that has occupied my attention for several years. I have been
looking for factors that, over the centuries, have determined the
outlook of Westerners on themselves and on the world; because
this outlook has a big influence on how we regard our chart components, and on how we evaluate and place them in our experience!
For example, if we arbitrarily dismiss fantasy and dreams as a lot
of unsubstantial nonsense, this will automatically result in the 12th
house being undervalued and the planet Neptune being less well
understood, to say nothing of Pisces. I am now going to produce
a historical and psychological scenario aimed at showing how we

have slowly formed a cultural judgment on the 12th house and have lost sight of its true nature.[11]

The Inheritance of Western Culture

Western society and its values are rooted in Jewish and Christian tradition. And whether we are believers or not, and whether or not our parents gave us a religious upbringing, our culture is pervaded by our religious inheritance. We carry its values in our share of the collective unconscious where it binds us to our culture. These values are certainly not statistical data stored in the unconscious, nor are they recollections of activities past and present. They are much much more. On the basis of these values, these opinions, these ideas, our forefathers acted, fought against certain things, acquired experience, and gained a specific outlook on life. Therefore, we are dealing not simply with the personal psyche, but with something that is rooted in our cultural pattern and in the convictions, behavior, ideas and repressions of our ancestors.

If something has been systematically repressed or rejected for generations, then we know for sure that it will figure more and more strongly in the unconscious; and that the more comprehensive and powerful the repression, the more archaic and primitive the level involved. To put it more clearly: the values prized by Jewish and Christian thought can be completely displaced by other values arising out of the unconscious if that concept persists in being one-sided and makes no attempt to integrate the shadow side of the concept. For only when you dare to remain open to the shadow side of your convictions—a side which is always present—and dare

---

[11]I do not think that it was "Christian culture" that made people see the 12th house as something grim and forbidding. Manulius was writing the second book of the *Astronomica* in the reign of Augustus, who died when Jesus Christ was only 18 and, therefore, before Christianity started. In this second book, he describes the 12th house as "a temple of ill omen, hostile to future activity and all too fruitful of bane . . . with the spectacle of ruin before its eyes." (Translation by G.P. Goold, published for the Loeb Classical Library by the Harvard University Press, 1977). And Ptolemy called it the house of the evil demon. Thus it was the old pagans who taught us that the 12th is grim. Tr.

to give it a place and integrate it, will you be able to keep these values in balance. If you do not, then it is virtually inevitable for enantiodromia to occur, the principle according to which everything changes into its opposite.

In the epoch when Christianity arose, there was a need for the sort of "male thinking" that made possible a far-reaching development of our ego. Some say that this archetype began to take shape when Christianity started to spread, rather than at its very earliest stage, and cite the doctrine of the Trinity in support of this view.

In her treatise on alchemy, von Franz alleges that Christendom is clearly patriarchal in tendency, and that it associates the feminine principle with matter, and matter with the Devil.[12] She sees the feminine principle in the form of Eve involved with the Serpent and letting sin into the world—the feminine principle as witch. She also refers to early Gnostic texts that postulate a female goddess or feminine Wisdom accompanying God. They called her Sophia. Von Franz writes that there are one or two obscure references to a dark chaotic "mother-mass" in the Deep, identifiable with matter, and to a sublime female figure who represents the wisdom of God. But, in the meantime, this figure left the scene, and the matter was regarded as the Devil's domain. Emphasis was laid on the Holy Ghost, the Spirit of Christ in the Godhead.

The one-sided view of matter led to a further development that expressed itself in the opinion that nature (downgraded to matter) has no better purpose than to contribute to human welfare. Mystery, beauty and divinity vanished from nature, because people were losing contact with their own mystery and inner wisdom (their own Sophia). The mystery of nature that had been pushed into the unconscious was projected on nature in the form of fear; and so nature had to be dominated in order to neutralize its "threat." Nature was no longer seen as a meaningful whole. People had assumed the "right" to manage and slaughter animals on a large scale. The 20th century has seen the exploitation of natural resources culminate in massive over-cultivation, not only in Western lands but elsewhere in the world where Western models are grad-

---

[12]M.L. von Franz, *Alchemy: An Introduction to the Symbolism and the Psychology* (Toronto: Inner City Press, 1982).

ually being introduced. The turning point, the point at which the law of enantiodromia says: now the process must change into its opposite, is as good as reached. Through refusing to allow nature its own value, humanity has become a danger to itself. It has neglected, repressed or exploited its own inner nature, so strongly bound up with the feminine, or Yin side of things.

The further differentiation and development of the conscious ego in our culture, together with a growing ascendancy of the male principle, was given expression in the Council of Constantinople in 869. Up until that time, it was taught that human beings consist of body, soul and spirit. At this Council, the concept of spirit was replaced by a concept that can best be described as "reason that resembles spirit." Symbolically expressed, this was the herald of an increasingly mechanistic view of life, humanity and nature. Little by little, everything around us was seen in terms of *use* rather than *meaning*. Causes and effects were investigated, and things became less important for what they were in themselves. If it was impossible to discover their purpose or use (and the two were often regarded as being the same thing!) then they were valueless.

One of the problems faced by missionaries when they tried to Christianize the Scandinavian lands was the enormous resistance to the observance of the seventh day as a day of rest, as the Lord's day. They got fierce reactions; people said that work itself was holy, an end in itself, and so there was no day needed for the worship of God. God was worshipped in daily affairs! This is an attitude much closer to Yin sagacity than we now realize. It is the readiness to allow things to be themselves. There is a measure of mystery in everything for those with emotional and spiritual perception. Each thing has a certain significance and worth that is not derived from rational appraisal. Each thing may just *be*, without any description or assessment, without a lot of fuss and bother and without having to be pigeon-holed into some little category.

It makes a tremendous difference whether work is seen as divine and as a completely meaningful part of life, or as a method for obtaining financial security or a comfortable old age. When work is simply seen as a means to an end without any awareness of its indescribable value, it is turned into an obligation and a necessary burden. And when the mystery of life itself in everyday reality can no longer be experienced, the religious archetype within a person can seek another form of expression, such as the worship of things that have little to do with God. Money, security and the like can become surrogate gods and can make us work for them like slaves.

The prevailing tendency to see everything in terms of goals and reasons, has automatically degraded a number of things into purposeless activities. People have come to think that it is a waste of time to sit day-dreaming, and that if they enjoy themselves their pleasure must also be profitable. We rush around trying to save time and feel that our leisure occupations have to yield some sort of advantage. Even time becomes our enemy and waiting is experienced as uncomfortable because it has no goal; if we are compelled to wait anywhere we look for some way of killing time! Whatever has no goal or obvious use, or does not fit into a logical pattern, is frivolous and even "sinful." And that brings us to the following problem in our culture.

Sin and Guilt, Good and Evil

God, the Father in Heaven, has become exclusively associated with Goodness and Love, and has become more and more clearly seen as a Father who judges each of us righteously and punishes the sins we have committed. Evil is no longer thought of as a part of God; God no longer represents the combined polarity of good and evil, but embodies only one facet of this polarity. The Devil has come to represent the other facet: he is the evil one, the tempter, and unrighteous, lascivious, materialistic, destructive and a great deal more of the same kind. The gods in many other religions do possess duality: they give and take, and are constructive and destructive, each in their own terrain. Christianity knows nothing (in its orthodox form) of the union of good and evil in one God. Nevertheless, the church and society do have to meet the consequences of this dissociation. What are we to make of the Book of Job, in which we encounter God the Omniscient and Good as One who, in our eyes, does not seem to act with complete fairness, and even seems to be jealous?

God gave the West the Ten Commandments through Moses, as the God who lays down the law we must obey. In this respect,

God is seen as a Heavenly authority who is inviolable and may not be defied with impunity. An important process in the developmental history of humanity is that originally external values gradually become internalized. In other words, where we were originally subject to an authority experienced as being outside ourselves, we increasingly feel these commands as coming out of our own being without being conscious of the fact. In Jungian terms, the centuries-long specific attitude of obedience to the commands of a Heavenly authority becomes, for people born in this culture, a part of the collective unconscious, a part of their psycho-cultural inheritance. And so it operates from within and determines our behavior and attitudes, without our being particularly aware of it. This means that, at the present time, even the most hardened atheist can be motivated by values that stem from the beginning of Christendom, solely and simply because they are part of our culture.

One of the consequences of overemphasis on the power of the Heavenly Authority is the automatic undervaluation of the person as an individual with a separate personality. There can be a low opinion of ourselves, whether we are men or women, and considerable guilt feelings, in the unconscious. Generally speaking we are unaware of these facts (or, if we are, then it is with the head and not with the heart), but they do determine a large part of our conduct. In a world where the church and religion have lost much of their influence, the sanctions held by Heaven have been spontaneously projected onto the state for example. And so the moral values of society and of the state have become the standard for the still impersonal ego; and those involved in personal psychological development face a stiff fight with the generally accepted values, to the extent that sometimes they feel they really do not "fit in." However, the majority, irrespective of their level of education or their function in society, usually accepts patriarchal values. This can show itself in either of two ways: either God Himself is projected onto the state, which then can do no wrong and is always good (an attitude that some totalitarian states have carried to extremes). Or the devil is projected on the state, which is then regarded as corrupt, menacing, sick and generally evil. The representatives of the two groups are liable to be at daggers drawn.

But the feelings of unworthiness that we have cultivated unconsciously in our culture also produce other sorts of projection and behavior. It is no secret that many people try to overcompensate by showing off. Indirectly this leads to feelings of separatism and nonconformity: they must be better than their neighbors (and preferably outdo them), whereas the Christian culture preaches disinterested love of and help to our neighbors, without consulting our own self-interest.

For centuries we have sucked in with our mothers' milk that we are nothing but sinners before God. Sin and guilt have formed the basis of Judeo-Christian thinking, and some of our blackest sins involve giving way to instinctive drives that are a part of human nature. We feel guilty for being what we are—human. And being human implies the possession of instinctive drives, including aggressive tendencies, destructive urges, the need for power; all of which in their unfrustrated form are essential to sound functioning. By refusing to accept our human nature, we lump all instinctive drives together as bad.

When guilt feelings are associated with the instincts, it makes sense for us to deny our drives. Identification with good is more comfortable, especially when it brings recognition for us as good members of our group. But if we refuse to recognize these instinctive drives, and do not give them their rightful place, they will eventually develop into such powerfully unconscious energy fields that they will disrupt our conscious activities. Worse still, they can turn us into people who do the exact opposite of what we profess. Asocial behavior, strong egocentricity, egotistical actions taken under the cloak of goodness, an enormous lust for power behind the mask of doing what is best for others, and similar distortions are then much in evidence. But because we do not wish to see the forces that are playing a role in us, we see these things in others, and feel completely justified in judging them, condemning them, perhaps opposing them, punishing them or even driving them away. Others always embody the evil that threatens our upright life. But whatever we do, this evil will always keep crossing our path, because it is a part of ourselves. It will be obvious that people who live in Western society are all more or less in the same boat; and that we pass on to our children a message with a double standard of morality—a message that unmistakably shows in the 12th house of the child, as we have seen in earlier chapters.

Suffering, Pain and Error

That God is only Goodness and Love, has a further consequence. Suffering, pain, misery, setbacks, death, destruction, grief, ruin, are not things that belong to the reality of God in Christ, and must therefore be regarded as penalties or due to error, and as something that is neither given by nor belongs to God. These feelings are bereft of any divine value, of meaning and of their right to exist. They must be done away with. We see this in questions such as: "What have I done to deserve all this wretchedness?" or, "How, in heaven's name, am I going to get out of all these difficulties?"

But someone with a different attitude would enquire: "What is the significance of these events, what have they to say?" Or, "Which part of me is in the process of renewal or change?" Making up our minds to take things as they come, and accepting that pain and sorrow have a part to play in our lives, can open us up to the value of these things and therefore to their creative possibilities. This attitude can even help us to bear pain and assimilate sorrow.

Instead, most people view times of distress as a punishment; and, after some shocking experience, one can even hear faithful church-goers exclaim in a troubled way, "How could a God of love let this happen? Can there really be a God?" If God is only good, tragedy does not make sense in some; others call it the will of God, and take it on blind trust.[13]

In the sort of worldview I have described there is, as we have seen, no place for human suffering, pain or sorrow. Worse still, people feel that others are judging them on the quiet, and saying, behind their backs that the things they are suffering are their just deserts and evidence that they are guilty of something or other.

---

[13]The attitudes mentioned by the author are very common, but before we propose ourselves as suitable candidates for judging God, we need a very good character reference. I believe it was Paul Brunton in *A Search in Secret India* who tells of his complaining to a famous maharishi that he failed to see where the benevolent regard of the Deity came in, and of the displeasure of the guru at his remark. The maharishi simply looked at him and said, "As you are, so is the world." I think, too, that many Christians have more insight into the nature of good and evil than perhaps the author gives them credit for. In this respect, the chapter on "The Significance of Evil" in Professor C.E.M. Joad's book, *The Recovery of Belief* (Faber & Faber, 1952) might repay reading. Tr.

Those who become entangled in problems for some reason, are "kicked when they are down" with feelings of guilt and shame. No wonder that pain and grief are often treated as things to hide, and even banished, because they are in conflict with people's ideas about God. Failure and sorrow must be avoided at all costs. Pain may not be any part of normal living, and must be fought. Of course, I am not advocating that sufferers should be left to writhe in agony. This is not my intention. What I am talking about is the pain that life can give, including physical discomfort.

In many Western countries, for example, childbirth is almost seen as a form of disease, and in The Netherlands, pregnancy is jokingly referred to as the "healthy sickness." Thus the woman in labor has to be offered twilight sleep to make childbirth less painful, instead of being shown the meaning of the pains. Pain is a normal component of life, that has to be accepted as a signal. As my own midwife said so beautifully: "Think that each contraction is bringing you nearer to your child. . . ." With such an approach, pain feels completely different, and can no longer be called the usual pain. To yield to such a pain is a true yin art. Once again, I must stress that I am not opposed to anesthesia and pain-killers as such. There are numerous cases in which drugs are really helpful. What I am getting at is that, in our culture, which sometimes is mockingly called the aspirin age, the rule is to try and suppress every symptom of pain, and all pains are treated alike. No one should want to feel it, for fear of being dubbed a masochist. Pain-killing can be at the expense of our inner emotional wealth, and may deaden the psychic as well as physical feelings (and we may not even care, because we think our psychic feelings only create confusion and contribute nothing!). It may dull the psyche if we try to rid ourselves of discomfort and the symptoms. The message being conveyed by the pain, and the meaningfulness of the pain, is never going to reach us in this way. Various therapists, among them Arnold Mindell in his work with dreams and the body, have let us see how significant pain can be as an accompaniment of transformation processes.

We observe two completely different reactions to this general attitude toward pain and suffering. The first is a strong desire to do something about it and to remove everything bad: which, apart from everything else, can lead to genetic manipulation in order to produce happier individuals without flaws. Here we have two overcompensations from the unconscious: the sinful human being, for one thing, wants to sit on the throne of God and judge what is best and what is not. Everything that does not meet the norm of Goodness and Love is repressed, and the repressed material becomes so alarming that it is "put to fire and sword" under the banner of doing what is right.

And then, we have precisely the opposite reaction: where the right is not assumed to fight against ills, there is an acceptance of suffering in order to do penance. The line taken is that, being human, people must suffer to purify themselves in the sight of God. The repressed material of our culture is placed on a pedestal, but within the cultural norm: that we are all sinful and laden with guilt.

Both attitudes are characterized by restricting the living-space of the individual; which, in the first case must conform to a religious pattern even where the physical side of things is concerned, and therefore is so reduced that the individual cannot develop according to his or her nature, and, in the second case, is even more of a constraint on personal development, because anything that does not have to be suffered or sacrificed is prejudged as having no value. But even here, pain and suffering are not seen for what they are in themselves but are treated very subjectively.

Thus there is no real living-space for the individual, no genuine scope for divergence, for the dark and mysterious, for the "useless" and the passive, for pain and suffering, or in short for the yin and the female, either in man or woman. But it is the yin and the female qualities that create room, and an approach that is not so obsessed with usefulness; an approach where both pain and pleasure are acknowledged, where sorrow and suffering are accepted as a part of life and reality, as are demolition and destruction, which are prerequisites for new creation. Destruction and creation are two sides of the same coin, and in the yin lies the realization that transformation cannot take place with the retention of everything old.[14]

---

[14]The Judeo-Christian roots of our Western civilization to which the author refers puts out the same message as she does here. Thus the Jewish Bible book of Ecclesiastes, talks of there being a time for every purpose under heaven: ". . . a time to kill, and a time to heal; a time to break down and a time to build up; a time to weep, and a time to laugh . . ." And Jesus said, "Neither do men put new wine into old bottles." Tr.

Something always has to be demolished or destroyed before anything new can arise.

Responding to the rhythm of life, and going to meet life in an open and expectant frame of mind, with a willingness to be fructified by the moment and to experience joy and sorrow to the full without a sense of guilt, is a true feminine characteristic, a yin quality that has been lost in our culture. But now, in these times, these values in their extreme forms have come hammering at the gates of our bastions of consciousness. They want to be readmitted into our pattern of values in order to make for stability. Their return is inevitable because, after all, opposite values do exist. And the passive and the receptive, the fanciful and the dreamy, the dissident and less calculable, the aggressive and the delightful, want to take their place again, to mention only a few possibilities. Another attitude to life is required, an attitude of openness to things as they are, of acceptance of life as it comes. In other words, what is required is some surrender to life, without being governed by the impulse to control life in all its facets. We should learn to flow with the stream while remaining fully aware. For centuries, this attitude has been laid under a ban in our Western culture.

This receptivity and openness, this preparedness to go along with what happens and to see its creative side, is the feminine or yin principle in creation. This side is represented by the woman and by the feminine in the man. It is a misconception to regard it as passivity and inaction—a misconception that is prevalent in our culture. What we are talking about is a form of open involvement (an involvement, too, with other aspects of our links with life) where not-doing is as important as doing, although doing is not excluded by any means.

Edward Whitmont illustrates this very vividly in his book, *Return of the Goddess*, by means of a description of the way the female reproductive system and the egg-cell in particular operate on the male.[15] At first sight, one would say that the female is passive and receptive, but her behavior is also devouring. She has a relaxed openness as she prepares to receive. In sharp contrast to this relative stillness are the thousands of restless, swarming spermatozoa each with a single goal: to force its way into the ovum. (A further amusing

---

[15]E.C. Whitmont, *The Return of the Goddess* (New York: Crossroad, 1984).

detail is that, according to some biologists, the ovum may choose which male cell will penetrate it!) But, at this stage, the male is passive, not aggressive. It is a spent force, and the female activity now rises to the surface and subjugates the male. The male cell is taken inside the female cell and is broken down by enzymes to provide a source of materials for building a new organism, the embryo. And we note that, in this new beginning, the embryo is not a neuter compromise between male and female, as was once thought, but is female. In overcoming the male and refashioning him in her own likeness, the female herself is transformed. Although, on the outside, she seems receptive and subject to aggressive penetration, the fact is that, in her inner invisible mystery, she actively overcomes male resistance and strips the male of the substance she requires for her work of creation and renewal. At the same time, we see that, in her inner sanctuary, the outwardly aggressive male can experience the salutary effects of full submission to her unfamiliar wisdom.

This process illustrates that dismantling and liquidation are prerequisites for a genuinely new creation. Only these are life-renewing. However, the impulse to submit to the process is itself transforming and, armed with a new wisdom, the individual can go further. If the 12th house symbolizes anything, then it is this very process, this complete receptivity and readiness to take what comes, to integrate it and to use it as the germ of a new creation process, whether this takes shape in music, art, science or daily life. By this means, wisdom and inner wealth can be our portion, and when we need help doors can unexpectedly open for us. Deep down, in spite of pain and sorrow, life will be worth living.

8

The
Creative Power
of the Unconscious

Unplanned Yet Purposive

Of all the houses, the 12th has least affinity with planning and regulation. It has its own secret timetable, and surprises us with feelings, emotions, desires and circumstances, the origin of which is inexplicable. Radical planets connected with the 12th house (in the 12th or in aspect to the ruler of the 12th) always give us the feeling that we cannot control them, do not see into them clearly, and do not know what to make of them—as we have already seen in earlier chapters. So the 12th house is a problem, and is continually subverting our efforts to have everything cut and dried. From the point of view of our cultural background, this is the overriding objection to this house. "It is bad, because we can do nothing with it. It is bad, because it promotes inactivity and undermines conscious organization. It is bad because it demotivates people and encourages them to let things slide. It is bad because it is the house of secret enemies." Such judgments flow from our current cultural pattern. The latter encourages us to focus on the forms of expression of the 12th house and to miss its real nature.

Let us look at this concept from a different point of view. By daring to take things as they come, we find that in spite of their unpredictability, they often turn out well for us. If we interfere and try to control things, the very reverse frequently seems to happen! It is disconcerting to the conscious mind not to be able to foresee the course of events. But the unconscious finds ways to experience things that belong to us, that have a healing effect and can even support us socially. Our earlier example of the publisher with a strongly emphasized 12th house is a good instance of this. Without any special reason other than that he feels good about it and that the idea just came into his head, he can publish a book on a certain subject. Unable to shake off the impression that it is the right thing to do, he goes ahead, even though his conscious mind tells him that the market for books on that subject is very limited. It looks as if he is being dumb, but somehow that does not seem to matter. And what happens? The moment the work apears in print, journalists start penning interesting articles on the subject (without having read the book!), and a television program is devoted to the same subject. Yet the publisher is not to know that this will happen, when the desire to print the book seizes him. What he experiences as a personal wish, now looks as if it was a glimpse of the future. By following a hunch, without bothering about statistics and market research, he has a best-seller on his hands. And so this publisher keeps ahead by bringing out books on subjects that are about to catch the public eye; books that are trendsetters and point the way to future developments in the country or in society.

Of course, to stay with our publisher for a moment, not all his books are hits. But then, not all his books are conceived in this fashion. What we are talking about is that special indescribable feeling that makes an idea stick in the mind. It refuses to go away, although it is not usually irritating. A moment comes when the individual feels that the decision has already been made to do something, and there is something different about it. This is the crux of the matter. The secret is to let oneself be carried along on the stream of inner events, through which the future speaks through us via the unconscious. The writer who responds to such promptings may find that he or she has a best-seller tucked away inside, or a book that lays the groundwork for social developments that are, as yet, almost imperceptible. In fact, each one of us, whatever our field of activity, can become incredibly creative in this way; this privilege is not confined to artists.

Goethe frequently remarked that his poems came to him, and that he felt instinctively compelled, as it were in a dream, to write them down there and then. Having done so, he felt purified, and as he put it, released from an oppressive mental tension. What he says is very significant: it often has a healing effect if we pay heed to this irrational urge that wants to say something to us. In a manner of speaking, we perform psychotherapy on ourselves. These things may be more strongly marked in one person than in another, but they are an essential characteristic of the 12th house. However, if we deny these feelings, or if we attempt to channel the creative efforts of the unconscious into a 9-to-5 groove, we not only seal its source, but become more and more uncomfortable without knowing exactly why. It is as if we have cut ourselves off from an important curative force and producer of psychic balance.

What Goethe said in his last years to Peter Eckermann is very illuminating: that the highest forms of productivity, the most significant insights or concepts, each discovery, each great thought that bears fruit and has further consequences, can be considered personal to nobody and are higher than any earthly power. He said that human beings, as genuine children of God, ought to treat these things as unexpected gifts from Above, which should be received respectfully and with joyful thanks. These inspirations are related to the demonic which, with superior force, does with individuals what it will, while they surrender to it unwittingly, believing that they are acting on their own initiative. In such cases, we can often see certain individuals as an instrument of a higher World Ruler (or World Power), or as vessels used to convey divine influence. He said this because he had seen how frequently a single idea changed the character of whole centuries; and how a single individual, through personal expression, has stamped something on his time that is handed down to future generations, and is still active in them.

The Research of Otto Kankeleit

The physician Otto Kankeleit was so fascinated by the creative potential of the unconscious revealed to him in his medical practice and in everyday life, that he devised an original questionnaire and sent it to distinguished scientists, artists, musicians, writers, actors and architects.[16] Three of his questions were: "To what extent and in what way does your creative output spring from the unconscious?" And: "Do dreams or pictorial ideas or memories play any part in the creative process?" "Can you describe for me how the creative process goes on in you?" The answers that came back spoke volumes. Only one person denied the action of the unconscious; almost everyone acknowledged that the unconscious plays an important part. For some it was even a predominating part. In order to enable the reader to picture how it is experienced, I shall give a few examples.

The French psychotherapist and author Maryse Choisy describes in a letter what happened to her after a serious traffic accident in which she suffered a head wound and concussion of the brain. She underwent an operation, and remained in the hospital for two months. After four months, she still could not think coherently. She tried reading the proofs of a book she had written before the accident, but was unable to follow her previous train of thought. "It was as if my conscious intelligence had completely disappeared," she says, "yet during the same period I wrote, without knowing how, some 20 poems and a novel. They came into my mind of their own accord. Many reviewers even say that that novel is my best. It was inspired in a real state of grace."

She goes on: "At the end of six months, logical thought returned, and I lost my state of grace, with its ease and spontaneity, and was completely deprived of the art of writing automatically. I have been unable to retain the spontaneity with logical thought. As intelligence returned, direct knowledge receded. . . . Also in 1944, three months after the accident and as soon as I returned home, I began to paint a lot. I had painted before, but the pictures were more labored and, like my literary work, very deliberate. I

---

[16]O. Kankeleit, *Das Unbewusste als Keinstätte des Schöpferischen. Selbrsterezeugnissen von Gelehrten, Dichtem und Kunstlern.* Munich, 1958.

always knew what I wanted before I started, and worked to a pre-conceived design. But, after the accident, I just dipped my brush into the colors at random and, as soon as I applied them to the canvas, I had the impression that a power beyond myself was guiding the brush. I did not feel responsible for my painting. And yet, the critics agree that my art in this condition was superior to my normal art. It was much more original and modern."

What would have happened if this lady had not engaged in writing and painting? Would she still have been able to experience the salutary power of the unconscious? She was cut off from her professional life for more than six months, but a great deal happened during this period. She speaks of a state of grace that disappeared when her normal intellectual capacity returned. But she could not hold on to both states of consciousness. I strongly suspect, however, that someone who had come to terms with their 12th house would be better able to combine the two worlds.

The philosopher, Prof. Gerhard Frei of Switzerland, writes: "As far as anything can be said about creative processes in the preparation of numerous lectures and articles over the last 25 years, my experience is approximately as follows: as soon as I know that I have to deal with a certain subject—perhaps a month later—it begins to work inside me. Not a day goes by when I am not consciously or half-consciously busy with the topic; and I am amazed how often books or articles I did not know existed suddenly come to hand to help me at the right moment. It makes one think of Jung's synchronicity. Frequently, I read something on a certain theme well in advance, make a note of it, and digest it quietly. As the date when it will be needed approaches, the whole thing suddenly stands before my eyes, logically arranged and divided. . . ."

Here is a splendid example of someone being creatively active while letting the process take its course. The doors that open of their own accord, already mentioned in the previous chapter, are represented here by the books and articles that inexplicably make their appearance at the right time.

Mathematician, Prof. Helmut Hasse, of the University of Hamburg, gives his account of what happens: "People think that mathematical truths are discovered by logical thought processes. But this is certainly not always so. The greatest and most epoch-making mathematical discoveries are first glimpsed with the inner eye, just as a work of art, before it is begun, is visualized in its entirety by the creative artist. And as the artist does not give it shape according to rules of the craft until this total view has been seen mentally, so the mathematician does not embark on a logical demonstration of some truth before recognizing it intuitively. The guideline for this recognition of a mathematical truth is, in many cases, the beauty of mathematical truth and the way in which it harmonizes both internally and with what is already known. You will have to take my word for this. I myself have experienced it in mathematical work of mine that has earned most approval from my professional colleagues. . . ."

Hasse adds another element to the picture: the beauty and harmonious relationship both within the theory and with what was known previously. Solutions contributed by the unconscious and brought into our minds by the action of the 12th house, are very often marked by their simplicity and by something that is indeed experienced as beauty.

The physicist, Prof. C. F. von Weizsäcker, of the Max Planck Institute in Göttingen, writes: "When I know that I have to work on a certain problem in a certain field, I realize that a great deal of conscious work and concentration is required; as likely as not exceeding my own strength. My own efforts never produce a breakthrough, but only a certain amount of spadework along conventional lines. By concentrating hard, I slowly burn myself out, like a small fire. But if I can then manage to relax properly (for minutes or, if necessary, for days or months), I find that in certain circumstances at an unexpected moment, such as in the morning when I awake, I get an inspiration that more or less answers the problem concerned. Afterward, I have to concentrate again; this time on interpreting the inspiration for the understanding. . . . Occasionally, an inspiration of this sort formulates or announces itself in a dream. Now and then, too, it takes the form of images, although not predominantly so. Time and time again I find myself repeating internally certain thoughts or words on which everything turns, although I do not at that time know what it is."

If one is really involved in a subject but is able to let it rest, there will be a sort of incubation period before it rises to the surface again. And when it does, a lot has happened to it in the meantime; much more than could ever have been achieved with diligent conscious work. The unconscious, however, can speak to us best at moments when the conscious is not intent on all sorts of matters. Therefore, those situations where you are not thinking of anything in particular—when you are taking a bath or shower, or sitting in the bathroom, absent-mindedly washing dishes, falling asleep or waking up, to name but a few—offer ideal moments for getting a flash of insight from the unconscious, which can then be further elaborated. Here we see the active male (see the last part of the previous chapter) penetrating the unconscious and becoming outwardly passive. Conscious attention to, and concentration on, the subject ceases. Meanwhile, the unconscious takes the matter up, transforms it, and creates something new out of it; after which it returns to the conscious! Deliberate control of the process would not achieve this!

The American writer, Pearl S. Buck says: "Each novel begins with a person who possibly originates in a problem or idea I have been thinking about for a long time. One person collects two or three others and, in my imagination, these come to life individually and together. I see how they move and how they talk to and live with one another. When they have been with me for some time, sometimes long, sometimes short, one of them steps forward and begins to speak in characteristic words. As soon as this happens, the novel comes alive and I start writing, preferably daily. . . ."

Here there is no conscious decision or carefully laid plot, but a manner of working that leaves the unconscious all the room in the world to be creative. The main character comes into existence of itself, and the process is rather like Jung's active imagination, which we shall examine in chapter 10.

Pearl Buck's horoscope is shown in chart 5 on page 98. She has Saturn in the 12th: very constructive for someone who allows the pattern of her narrative to emerge of itself. Saturn is also the ruler of the 4th house, so that she has the ruler of the 4th in the 12th. In daily life this often goes with a feeling of being displaced, and of not feeling at home in one's family or in the land where one lives. The sense of displacement is quite clearly expressed in her work, for example in her famous book, *East Wind, West Wind*.[17] It

---

[17] Pearl S. Buck, *East Wind, West Wind* (New York: John Day Books, 1973). Pearl Buck is best known for her novel, *The Good Earth*.

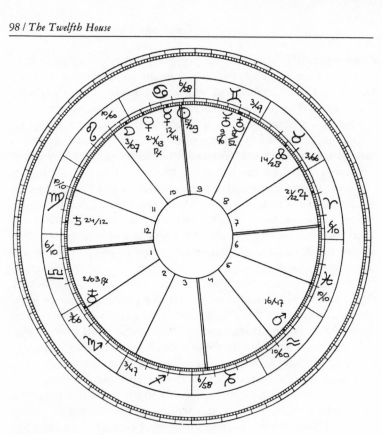

Chart 5. Natal chart of Pearl S. Buck, born June 26, 1892, Hillsboro, West Virginia, at 12:30 P.M.

is entirely possible that, by elaborating this theme as a writer, she was able to deal with her own feelings and, what is more, was able to impart a great inner strength to her books. Letting go and allowing things to happen in herself was an essential working method for her, a method by which she could adopt an attitude to the external world (ruler of the 12th on the MC) and with which she was able to identify well (ruler of the 12th conjunct the Sun).

Finally, here is an excerpt from an article written by the famous conductor, Prof. Eugen Jochum, and titled *Zur Phänomenologie des Dirigierens* (The Phenomenology of Conducting). "What I usually do initially is to adopt what one may call a passive attitude toward the work, with openness and freedom from bias, so that the composition can unfold its own reality. . . . In this way, the tempo takes care of itself and the piece expresses itself so naturally (through and out of itself), that it starts to live its own life. My conscious willpower and my formative impulses do not enter in at this stage. However, this apparently passive state seems to consist of several layers. Only the intellectual layers of the consciousness are really passive, and only the possessive, formative will is switched off. In contrast, the deeper layers of the conscious are extremely vibrant and active, and intent on the work, to the extent that a sort of emotional forcefield is created enabling the sparks to fly. This moment is decisive. When it is reached, conscious effort has to begin in a very painstaking way. The important point is that the will and conscious control do not enter into the process too early, and that my own personality does not interfere in the wrong place. Ethically, the attitude is one of humility toward the music as a whole, and of listening to its inner meaning."

Once again we see that the withdrawal of consciousness and the acceptance that something is going on inside over which one exercises no control can lead to the greatest results.

The horoscope of Eugen Jochum is known too. As we see from chart 6 on p. 100, his 12th house is strongly emphasized, and even afflicted. The Moon stands on the cusp of the 12th and the ruler of the 12th (Pluto) makes a Yod-aspect with the Moon and Saturn. Other aspects of the ruler of the 12th are an opposition to Uranus and a trine to Mercury. There is also a connection between Saturn and the 12th house, just as in Pearl Buck's chart. Just as she said that the structure of her novels arose spontaneously, so the tempo of Eugen Jochum takes care of itself. He also remarks that he does not add his own formative impulses to start with; the piece of music has to find its own voice initially. Formative forces are specially associated with the Moon and Saturn and, upon examination, we find that these two make a Yod-aspect with the ruler of the 12th! The field of tension in a Yod-aspect, and its uncertain, wary and questing qualities, can make one talented if one will dare to listen to the inner voice, and will dare to wait and to be vulnerable. The combination of this Yod with the 12th house has made Eugen Jochum one of the finest conductors of this century!

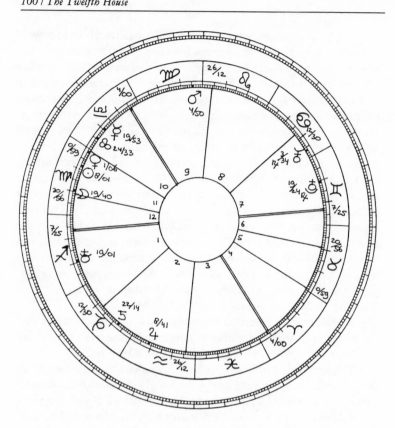

Chart 6. Natal chart of Eugen Jochum, born November 1, 1902, Babenhausen, West Germany, at 10:00 A.M.

The above examples with their different experiences and different points of view, show us how worthwhile it is to surrender ourselves to this influence that we can neither see nor control, but asks of us the patience to wait for an answer. This influence of the unconscious can, when we are receptive toward it, help us through very difficult periods, provided we relinquish our fixation on whatever is bothering us. This is the role of the 12th house in our charts. On its own, the 12th house resolves nothing. When it is understood, its impulse to dismantle helps in the move toward a new life-situation or in the solution of the problem. This impulse affects us more dramatically when we cling to old patterns and wear a tight mask or, in other words, when we display too little psychic flexibility. Even so, the 12th house can be enriching; although we may see this only in retrospect, when we come to understand it. In the following chapters we shall look at how to adopt a positive approach.

9

Conscious Work
with the
12th House

Favorable Conditions

In our hustling and bustling society, where time is money and people fear that if they stand still they are going to be left behind, planets in the 12th and in aspect to the ruler of the 12th are easily repressed, because these planets can deploy their influence satisfactorily, and so come into their own only when certain conditions are fulfilled. And these conditions are at odds with current trends. For example, the 12th house is the house of dreams and dream symbolism. Insight into and understanding one's dreams can provide powerful support in everyday life. But time has to be spent recalling them. If, when the alarm clock rings in the morning, you jump out of bed (without the leisure even to turn over, because you have set the clock to ring as late as possible) and head for the front door in order to be on time for work, your dreams will vanish without trace. But if you lie dozing for a while, quiet and relaxed, there is a fair chance that snatches of what you have been dreaming, or even a whole dream, will enter consciousness.

Try to assimilate what comes to the surface, and possibly keep a dream journal, so that the things dreamed over a period will reveal what themes are occupying the unconscious, themes you might otherwise remain unaware of. As the unconscious is certainly not a receptacle of misery, but a psychological factor that forms a splendid counterpart to the conscious and can help it in all sorts of ways, dreams are among the most important sources of knowledge of what the unconscious actually contributes.

The half-conscious state between waking and sleeping, when we are quiet and relaxed, is a situation in which the 12th house can all at once become noticeable and even active. Also any situation in which we are very relaxed and not under stress—but receptive and free from the desire to do things—is a good opportunity for experiencing the power of the 12th house. In fact, we could say that the 12th house comes into its own whenever we are ready to take life as it comes and quietly accept whatever offers itself either from within or from without, in general whenever we are not worried about time and when we are not trying to anticipate what will happen. Instances of this are day-dreaming over the sink, slumbering before going to sleep, or as we are beginning to wake up, watching a fishing-float at the end of the rod and line, sitting in the bath, standing vacantly in the street or in the house, strolling gently through the woods or along the sea shore, and so on. The possibilities are numerous and the 12th house is always active in such cases. But if we pay no attention to what it has been telling us and act as though the time of relaxation had never happened, the messages of the 12th house fly away and it remains as mysterious as before. I have frequently observed that people with Uranus in the 12th, or in aspect to the ruler of the 12th have a sort of underlying nervousness. Something inside them is constantly on the alert. People like this can have the most marvelous inspirations at the most unpredictable moments, or can gain insight into a problem in a flash. But . . . not by sitting down and thinking about it. By trying to force themselves to find a creative answer to problems during their working hours, they will only make themselves tense and restless without achieving anything useful. Their restlessness mystifies them. If they study themselves (knowing how Uranus works in connection with the 12th house), they will notice a surge of fantasy while they are shaving or washing their faces in the morning, or that the answer to a knotty problem comes out of the blue when they are caught in a traffic jam and are vacantly gazing about them.

It is in the more idle moments of the conscious mind, when it is not working at top speed, that intuitive and extremely valuable pieces of advice emerge from the unconscious. Therefore if you have such a placement or aspect of Uranus, do keep a writing pad in your bathroom or near your bed, stuff a notebook in your bag or case, or keep a dictaphone in your car as I do, and you will find that after a time you will accumulate some remarkable insights and ideas, some of them literally golden.

Every planet in the 12th or in aspect to the ruler of the 12th can provide sudden help if only you will create conditions that suit the 12th house. For one thing, being alone can be important, because when we are alone most of us feel less pressurized and more inclined to let go. Nevertheless, this does not imply that people with a heavily tenanted 12th house (or with any aspects to the ruler of the 12th) are lazy when on their own; on the contrary, they are usually active and seldom bored! Anyway, seclusion is always an opportunity for the inner life to make itself felt. And if you are prepared to welcome this side of yourself cheerfully, the 12th house need not become a source of any great anxiety (see the opening chapters).

In preparing the ground for the 12th house to develop, we can proceed in one of two ways:

A) By using (as a deliberate technique for discovering and getting to know the 12th house) one of the methods by which the unconscious announces itself. Among other things, the 12th house becomes active in dreams, meditation, fantasy, association and active imagination. We can employ one or more of these techniques in order to examine the significance for our psyche of a planet in the 12th or in aspect to the ruler of the 12th. Because fantasy and active imagination belong to the 12th house, we have in theory an endless number of methods available to us: when the 12th house is open, we can easily find our own ways to contact the unconscious, and quite often these ways occur to us spontaneously.

B) By applying the methods used for accessing the 12th house to other factors in the horoscope, in order to find the bottlenecks in our characters through the language of symbol and imagery. Once we succeed in this, without the agency of the conscious will or guiding ego, creative solutions for the problems implicating these other horoscope factors will emerge from the unconscious. Possibly these will be solutions that the conscious mind would never have devised or opted for, and may even fill it with doubt. But if the contact with the unconscious is honest enough (more of this later), it will be found in retrospect that the solution was perfectly sensible. It has to be realized that the unconscious is not concerned with things the conscious finds important. Thus, for the psyche as a whole, it can be vital to take a step backward in life if we are to continue to function satisfactorily, even while the conscious mind is thinking of advancing. Those who let the 12th house have its say are more sensitive to the needs of the total psyche and are in a better position to restore their vital balance.

We shall go into this more deeply in the following paragraphs.

Working with 12th House Planets

So what can be done constructively with planets in the 12th and in aspect to the ruler of the 12th? I asked my class members at two evening sessions to go home and think about this question, so that we could discuss it on a third evening. It was surprising how people kept dwelling on bad experiences, and on how negatively the matters connected with the 12th house had turned out at times. There were not many testimonies to the constructive operation of these planets. Often, people would refer to the general circumstances of the 12th house. The most frequently mentioned positive aspects were service to others, religious experience, social work, personal involvement in aid to the third world, art, the ability to keep a sense of proportion, and the feeling of oneness with life and with the rest of the universe.

It might seem that with any planet in the 12th house, the native is sensitive, compassionate, fond of walking in the woods, and dogged by feelings of uncertainty. The nature of the planet, however, does make a substantial difference. The native has to overcome a lack of familiarity with other ways of looking at life in order to act constructively. It is not so much that he or she will be the sort of person who likes walking through the woods as, that by walking through the woods a 12th-house situation is created that encourages the planet concerned to express itself. But this is just a beginning. Of course you will feel happy with the psychic factors that are linked to the 12th house when you are wandering through a wood. Any circumstance that suits the 12th house can have a favorable effect on 12th-house planets. But each planet has a specific way of showing itself.

If you want to be constructive, immerse yourself, to begin with, in the nature of the planet. Look at the things that connect it with the external world. Create a peaceful atmosphere from which haste and pressure and getting things done are excluded and give the planet time. Let us suppose you have Mercury in the 12th. Outwardly, Mercury has to do with writing, with pen and paper, with drawing, versification and puzzles; also with brief contacts, short excursions, trade and traffic, to mention but a few possibilities. Now do something belonging to this planet in a 12th-house mode. Take pen and paper, say, and start writing without any fixed plot in mind. Do not try to improve anything, but accept what comes. Or sit and draw. Or catch the bus and submerge yourself, by yourself, in the seething crowd of busy shoppers. Expect nothing; just wait and see what happens. As likely as not nothing particularly great or strange will occur; and yet, one idea follows another (Mercury again).

As you continue sketching, maybe something you would never have expected and perhaps do not understand emerges—or not, as the case may be. If you write a little story, it may seem to be completely bungled or may not be bad. Either way, simply leave it. Next day (or next week) resume the activity. If you do this regularly, you will notice (usually on looking back on it) that it undergoes a change. For example, in writing, your subject becomes more complex. And, without your having discussed it with anyone, a good book comes into your hands—a book on precisely that subject. Or you switch on the radio right in the middle of a talk on that very subject. It is as if something mysteriously resonated with your thoughts.

All this takes longer for some than for others. Time plays no part in the unconscious, which is completely unpredictable. What is more, some of us have a barrier to pass, because we find it rather novel to sit idly writing or drawing. "I cannot just sit down and start writing or drawing!" is a common objection. Never mind—

go and do it! If you feel uncomfortable and inhibited, it is only a sign that the 12th-house processes are getting under way rather slowly.

It can be pleasant to work with any 12th-house planet. And there is no need for frantic activity. Possibly you will immerse yourself in something. Thus Saturn in the 12th or in aspect to the ruler of the 12th can indicate a fondness for old crafts and materials: clay, stone, wood, leather, etc. There may also be an interest in trees, fossils and prehistory, skeletons, and architecture. With this in mind, take a piece of wood or a lump of clay and quietly set to work without any preconceived pattern or plan. Simply follow the inner impulse. After several attempts, you will notice that these activities have a calming effect, and that you enjoy deep relaxation. If you are able to surrender yourself to them completely, you may feel yourself soaring serenely above all the little everyday anxieties. Tension of which you may not have been aware is removed, leaving you with the realization that it has always been there. To immerse yourself in the 12th house, as if losing yourself in another world, is a process that creates much more inner balance than might at first be supposed.

A feeling of oneness with others is a 12th-house quality we can actively employ with various planets there. A connection between the Sun or Mars and the 12th house can in itself make you afraid to stand up for your rights. With the Sun, this is due to an identity problem; with Mars, it is due more to the fear of getting into a fight. In either case, direct confrontations are felt to be very menacing. But if you can create a situation in which the menacing aspect of confrontation is pushed into the background, and the feeling of unity and perceptiveness of the 12th house can play a larger role, then you can do well in such pursuits as studying martial arts. The latter demands a perfect awareness of the movements and thrusts of the opponent: it is essential to know exactly when to give way and when to strike. There is no time for reflection in such a combat. In other words, it is essential to be able to pick up the slightest signal, which is sensed rather than objectively seen, and to yield to the flow of events. Genuine talent is shown in this surrender to the moment, and in the feeling of unity with the opponent and with the contest as a whole. With an aspect between the Sun and/or Mars and the 12th house, you are able to let your being (the Sun) and fighting spirit (Mars) merge into a unity with others and with the moment.

There is always a lurking danger in the 12th house, and this is the danger of going to extremes, the danger of alcoholism, or the danger of some other addiction. But it is not only drink and drugs that come under the rulership of the 12th house. It represents all forms of addiction by which the personality can be under-mined—including addiction to a religious institution or person (e.g., a guru), to the intoxication of engaging in a certain activity (e.g., running the marathon), and so on. As with everything to do with the 12th house, it is impossible to draw sharp distinctions. An artist who strikes a 12th-house vein of creative activity, and hardly sleeps for weeks, eats very little, and can think of nothing but what he or she is making at the moment, suffers a form of addiction from which recovery takes place as soon as the "fit" is over. (Actually, some of this exceptional personal creativity stems from the 8th house; but the atmosphere and the intoxication surrounding it come from the 12th).

If we have found activities in everyday life that we feel tran-quilizing, there are some further advantages. In the first place there is a good likelihood that the matters associated with planets in the 12th and in aspect to the ruler of the 12th will become less stressful or will arouse less anxiety, because they now have a safety valve and integration potential in their own sphere. In the second place, these 12th-house factors can be enormously stimulating to us when we are alone. In the third place, they are connected with a level in us that is not limited by time and space, and can give us ideas that are futuristic. And, finally, when the 12th house as a whole is allowed the opportunity to develop, it is much easier to employ general 12th-house techniques and methods in order to restore equilibrium and promote psychic growth.

All techniques and activities by which the conscious ego retires to some extent and surrenders itself in an open mode to what it neither knows nor understands, to the world of the non-rational within or without, have to do with the 12th house. This means that mental states such as dreaming and fantasizing are extremely helpful for contacting the 12th house. In addition, we can have recourse to meditation and prayer, hypnotism and active imagination, as-sociation experiments, religion and the collective wisdom found in fairy tales, myths and legends. Also, activities involving energies not recognized by Western science, but nevertheless apparently perfectly capable of acting on and in the human body, have a 12th-house component. Examples are homeopathy, acupuncture, shiatsu, foot reflexology, reiki, yoga, and much more. Submitting to these, either actively or passively, gives the unconscious the chance to be constructive. However, there is the proviso that one must be willing to accept all the processes of change that irrevocably accompany them; otherwise the techniques will be sterile, and the indescribable, almost paranormal, fine sensitivity of the 12th house will never be developed. Moreover, the person who is so busily engaged in looking for the 12th-house cures and ignores the reality of daily life, is liable to fall prey to the enslaving and undermining tendencies of the 12th house.

By gaining insight into the 12th house and into the power of the collective unconscious that it symbolizes, the factors represented by those elusive planets that are bound up with this house can be brought to the surface. And we can use it to activate and influence all the other areas in our charts. However, the 12th house is not static; in each lifetime the dynamic relationship between the conscious and the unconscious brings different possibilities, and in each lifetime we can make varied use of the 12th house.

The 12th House at Different Stages in Life

The young child is immersed in a mythological world, a world in which lifeless objects can speak and act. It is a part of this world and at one with everything in it, and takes it completely for granted. Also taken for granted are invisible playmates. Almost every child has an invisible friend it involves in its everyday life. How many parents are there who have not had to lay an extra place at the table, so that the little friend can share the meal? For the child, the playmate is quite visible and tangible; for the adults it is not. The companion need not have human form, but may equally well be an animal—a cat, say, or even a crocodile. In this imaginary company, the child has wild adventures and endless games, and can release its emotions and react to things.

We should certainly not dismiss such an invisible playmate, the denizen of the child's imagination, as nonsense or infantile prattle. To the child it is perfectly real; and, psychologically speaking, is even a healthy sign. What happens is that the child is projecting something of itself on the world; something with which to operate. The game teaches how to deal with external situations and with the things of daily life. If the child is scolded for leaving half its food on its plate, it can speak crossly to the imaginary friend for doing the same, and so create an inner balance between the action of the parent(s) and its own passive role. It has switched over to becoming the active party. The same thing happens with children and their dolls and toy animals. Again there is a projection, in which the object is "brought to life" so that the child can come to terms with existence.

Giving active rein to fantasy, making up stories, experimenting with problems and difficulties in play, in drawing, in dancing, and so on, is very important for achieving balance. The fantasy, the absorption in play, so that time and self are both forgotten, the obliteration of the distinction between dream or fantasy and reality, all belong to the 12th house.

The child who leaves the mythic phase slowly and is gradually confronted with more and more of what we call reality, will be better placed to draw the line between this physical reality and the world of fantasy. For many children, the transition means that life becomes less colorful and animated. Santa Claus or Father Christmas ceases to exist, you are unable to hear the trees and the stones, which must prove that they are unable to talk, and a plaything in your hand is more real than one in your thoughts. Hard facts have come closer.

The inwardly creative child will not bury his or her fantasy during this transition period. A child of this sort will keep its sense of wonder intact, and be able to appreciate both dreaming and ordinary reality. Fantasy will eventually be used for dreaming about the future: powerful visions in which the child, of course, is the hero or heroine. The child whose fantasy is not blocked in some way, will have a marvelous instrument at its disposal. Because in these dreams it lightly scans its own unconscious potential, which it then unfolds from within in a suitable direction, although without knowing what is going on. If it is not persuaded to dismiss fantasizing as stuff and nonsense, and if it does not have to pretend that it no longer fantasizes (because only small children do things like that), but regards dreaming and fantasizing as next in value to everyday life, then these will assist the child to become well-balanced and free from boredom. Behind the scenes they will prepare its way to the future.

A child who grows up with both feet firmly planted on the ground, and yet with plenty of room for rich inner imagery, quite often develops a "small voice" or a sixth sense, which reveals the answer to difficult situations. This child, who has remained open to the reality of the invisible world, takes the voice or sense seriously, though possibly wary of mentioning the matter to others. The adolescent or young adult who has learned to attend to the voice, and also to subtle signals from inside and outside, can easily recharge his or her batteries by listening to music, enjoying the peace of nature, and so on.

The same applies with equal force to building a career or starting a family. Generally the period is one offering very little rest and relaxation to the young adult: the pressure of work and of caring for children allows scant opportunity for such things. And yet the 12th house can make its presence felt, even during this busy time, provided one is open to it. We can share with our children such activities as drawing, painting, playing with modeling clay, dancing, and naturally—what was mentioned by nearly all my class members—walking in the woods and along the sea-shore! Nor must we forget the reading out loud of nursery tales.

Fairy stories, myths and legends have a deep eloquence, especially in their pure, and often raw, form. For they are not really improved by cutting out the unpleasant or grim episodes. Genuine fairy stories emerge from the collective unconscious. They state the problems of life and their solutions in symbolic guise. Imperceptibly, the telling of such stories has a salutary effect on children, and bestows on them a treasure store of lessons on life. A child's favorite tale, which may not be the same one at every age, can say a lot about the problems it is currently wrestling with. Of course, it is very easy to let our children listen to a series of nursery tales recorded on tape or compact disc; but that is not the 12th-house style, which seeks an inner point of repose. This is created especially when one of the parents does something as a shared interest with the child—in this case, reading a fairy story. The more involved the parents, the better is the atmosphere of the occasion. The child not only drinks in the words, but also unconsciously latches onto something of the pictures evoked in the parent's mind by the story. If, as a parent, you are absorbed in what you are reading, you will experience certain emotions. What they are will depend on the nature of the tale, but they will always arise. Which stories strike a chord in you, and which do you dislike? These symbolize your inner potential or your problems.

When parents and children immerse themselves together in the world of fairy stories and myths, there is a stirring into activity of certain unconscious factors that can be very significant in the further development of the adult's personality. But the parent does have to enter into the spirit of the thing, sharing the enjoyment of the story, and maybe helping to draw some illustrations of it afterward. There will be no satisfaction in it, if the story is read absent-mindedly; and closeness to the child and the good after-effects will be missed. But then there are all sorts of likely, and unlikely, possibilities. Perhaps you like going to the movies or watching videos. What is your approach? You can become absorbed in films without paying much attention to the emotions they evoke. You can also amass a wealth of knowledge concerning the film world in a very factual way. The 12th-house method, however, is to become absorbed in certain films or scenes, so that you feel something being released inside you, and then to retain those feelings and allow them to work on you. Do you feel that the scenes should have ended differently? Why not use your imagination to create a variant of the film? Yes, and then try to work out what lies behind what you have done, and what was the part played by your emotions. By becoming involved in the story and by taking your feelings seriously, you give the 12th house a further opportunity to hint at a direction for you to take in life.

The woman who likes doing needlework can make allowances for her 12th house. She can simply begin without a pattern and wait for the design to emerge of itself, for the colors to suggest themselves, experiencing what happens rather than forcing it. Suddenly, a motif appears. Sometimes a piece of embroidery produced by this means can release so much energy that it is as if the embroiderer is forced by an invisible hand to do as much of it as possible. There is a sort of intoxication with the sacred task which does not come from the rational mind, because it is not anything the rational mind would consider a useful chore. When the work is finished it may even be difficult to show it to others because it is associated with something very intimate and very precious. Or one can take an idea or symbol as the theme of a piece of embroidery, knitting, weaving, tapestry or the like. Astrologers could use a planet or zodiac sign; or, perhaps more to the point, a certain planetary placement or aspect from the horoscope. The result, if it was produced by free association, will be a true meditation device. It can also come about that after a certain length of time (how long it is impossible to say) the person will need to work on the same horoscope factors again. A new and entirely different design is created. This is quite understandable. People inevitably change with time, and in the very process of playing with this part of the self in a symbolic manner, you are likely to bring it to a new level.

Astrodrama is another way of using the horoscope in a 12th-house manner. Although drama is assigned by some to the 5th house, I definitely see 12th-house components in it. In working with authentic experience-astrology, you have to slip off your current mask as the ego retreats a little, and have to surrender yourself to what you feel. A special way of experiencing the natal chart is to apply active imagination to its various factors, as I shall demonstrate in the next chapter.

Therefore, where the 12th house is concerned, it does not matter so much *what* you do as the attitude you adopt when you do it. Letting go, being prepared to feel and experience, allowing yourself to be swayed by the atmosphere of the occasion, and being prepared to enjoy what occurs, without looking for success or any particular outcome, are important components of this attitude. Paradoxically, this attitude is one that can contribute to success; but the success comes of itself and is not engineered.

Such an attitude is important for the whole of adult life, if you are to take advantage of what the 12th house has to offer. How that attitude is achieved is of minor importance. It may spring from meditation or from getting rid of your pent-up aggression in a wild and uninhibited dance, it may arise by taking a bath or by devotion to people or animals in need, so that self becomes relatively unimportant. These are all means of achieving that openness in which you accept life and also go to meet it, whether it is bright or dark.

For older folk, contact with the 12th house can mean sensing the source in themselves together with their oneness with life and its inescapable concomitant, death. They can now gather the fruit of the animated world in which they lived as children. And although they had to leave it behind in order to earn a living and raise a family, here, in the last phase of life and at the high point in the development of their consciousness, they can return with full awareness to the mythical phase. In this phase, life is inspired in a different way, seeing that the ego moves back a little. There is a maturity that enables us to take a more objective view of ourselves and to place ourselves in relation to life. Older people like this seem to radiate love and warmth somehow or other and, without saying anything, quietly shine as a beacon for those around. Not that they have to sit still, for often the last phase of life is the phase when people come into their own! The quietness of the 12th house is mainly an inner peace and rest.

In my opinion, the 12th house plays an incredibly important part in what Jung calls the process of individuation, the growing process in which, through setbacks and recoveries, we move nearer to our own being and the discovery of the self. As soon as we shut off the source of supply in the (collective) unconscious, true growth ceases and we become badly oriented to external things, because we cannot connect them with what is going on inside us. The chance that anxieties and phobias (which are other sides of the 12th house) will develop, is greater when the unconscious is blocked than when it maintains a living exchange with the conscious. This, however, does not imply that we are protected from depressions, anxieties and phobias by working with the 12th house. Even those who are most open to it have temporary problems. Besides, it is theoretically an error to think that, by doing things right, we shall earn the reward of freedom from anxiety more or less at once. This may be the conscious mind's idea of what should happen, but it is not the unconscious mind's idea. Depressions, anxieties and even chronic phobias can be signals from the unconscious that there is something inside us wanting to express itself and that we are keeping it out of conscious awareness. To the conscious, this may not make sense, but to the total psyche the sense it makes is excellent.

We must not make the mistake of judging those with a depression or phobia as if we were God. Even depressions or a series of fears and phobias are symbols by which the 12th house endeavors to express something; this time more in its dismantling quality. But through the same house we can gain access to these symbols and learn to understand why we have had a given experience. I have frequently heard people who have overcome severe depression or a phobia say that they suddenly had a very "clean" feeling—as if a lot had been worked out.

10

Active Imagination and the Horoscope

The Symbolic Language of the Unconscious

The language in which the unconscious speaks to us is colorful and symbolic. Everything is possible and it says nothing of restrictions or boundaries. Just as a dream can take unexpected twists and turns that would be impossible in real life, so can other manifestations of the unconscious; they have a dreamlike, fairy-tale quality. A dream can be disagreeable and threatening, irrational, alarming, gruesome and bloodthirsty or, on the other hand, ethereally beautiful, emotive, and full of warmth.

The plot of a dream or story can strike a chord in us or make our flesh creep. One way or another, the imagery in which it is clothed always stirs up a certain emotion, and the unconscious works on us internally, via the feelings evoked. The pictures, characters and narrative are none other than symbols for activities going on inside. They represent an attempt by the unconscious to say something to the conscious, but in a language the latter may find enigmatic. Thus the approach of a fit of depression can be forecast by a dream about swimming in a dark and dangerous lake, with the swimmer struggling to keep his or her head above water. Such a dream is seldom literal, apart from the occasional paranormal one: what it usually does is express something at work in us that has not yet penetrated consciousness.

People populate our dreams. They can be known to us, but some we have never met. Those whom we know represent, in the vast majority of cases, factors in ourselves, and are no more than convenient pegs on which to hang the latter. In the first place, a dream tells us something about ourselves. Important psychic contents, processes and repressions, but also hidden gifts, often seem to be personified. That is to say, in dreams about a certain person, a subjective factor or process is being represented, and the situation surrounding the person in the dream can provide indications about the status of this factor or process in ourselves.

This is an important consideration in Jungian psychology; but in other areas of psychology also, experiences are described that show how easily unconscious factors present themselves in human form. The American psychotherapist, M. G. Edelstien, writes in his book[18] about how he put his hypnotized patients in contact with the parts of themselves responsible for involuntary behavior, for compulsions and vicious circles difficult for the conscious mind to overcome. Edelstien found that almost each part in an individual has a name, and that it will state it when asked to do so. Sometimes the names are abstract, like "Punisher" or "Adventurer," but they may equally be "Sam" or "Mary." In many cases, patients have no idea where these names originate; they just pop up. The parts also have their own age and sex. In short, it is as if another, relatively autonomous personality is living inside the patient and has its own name, character, and behavior. Edelstien lets his patients converse with these parts in order to discover what the interior personalities want and why they are forcing the conscious personality to do things against its will. In the conversation between the patient and his or her inner part, a conversation that can be conducted like one between two individuals, there is often the possibility of reaching a compromise. Afterward, even if no compromise has been worked out, the patient's symptoms may be relieved to some extent.

In his work on transpersonal psychology, Ian Gordon Brown

---

[18]M.G. Edelstien, *Trauma, Trance & Transformation: A Clinical Guide to Hypnotherapy* (New York: Brunner-Mazel, 1981).

has also encountered what he calls subpersonalities. Howard Sasportas has successfully applied the recognition of and working with subpersonalities to the horoscope, as described in *The Development of the Personality*.[19] In fact he uses a 12th-house method on the horoscope that reminds us of what Edelstien did with hypnosis, and what Jung did in another way with active imagination. It is completely unimportant what theory is adopted when we "enter into a conversation" with our horoscope. What is central is the employment of a 12th-house technique to get in touch with personified factors that seem to be so marvelously represented by the radical configurations and planetary placements. Jung's active imagination technique seems to be a good instrument. The method has been further refined over the years by Jungian therapists. Since this technique not only fits in well with work on the horoscope, but is equally suitable for tackling any other area of life, I shall discuss it more in depth soon as an example of how a 12th-house technique can be applied to the horoscope, and to give anyone who wants to apply such a technique in this way a practical guide.

Active Imagination

Carl Jung, who in 1916 began with what he was later to call active imagination, describes it as a "dialectical discussion with the unconscious in order to reach agreement with it." It amounts to the active evocation of images that represent inner facts. Jungian psychology starts from the premise that our total psyche is perfectly aware of what is going on inside us, and that the unconscious mind can express this in pictures, fantasies, moods, melodies, emotions, feelings, and so on. The unconscious, however, is certainly not static, and its imagery does not take the form of "stills." And even though the conscious mind is not totally *au fait* with what is going on, generally speaking, the pictures, sounds or emotions that rise spontaneously to the surface are constantly changing; the processes are dynamic, as in daydreaming over the sink. All sorts of things are happening inside us; but we must not allow the conscious to

---

[19]L. Greene & H. Sasportas *The Development of the Personality* (York Beach, ME: Samuel Weiser, 1987; London: Arkana, 1989).

lay down a line for the internal narrative to follow. The only things of value are those that surface in our minds spontaneously. And the conscious must pay strict attention to what does surface in this fashion.

Many people find the first steps on the path of active imagination creepy or frightening. For a start, many people mistrust the unconscious on the mistaken grounds that it is nothing but a storehouse of misery. Others think that the unconscious is downright dangerous and that we must be crazy to have dealings with it. Because, in the initial steps taken in our encounter with the unconscious, we are quite likely to come into contact with the less pleasant sides of ourselves, it is easy to get the impression that the unconscious spells nothing but trouble. On the other hand, there are those who so canonize the unconscious that the conscious mind can get nowhere near it. This, too, is an unbalanced situation that hinders the development of the personality. Be all this as it may, the unconscious is definitely not dangerous and it will harm us only if we approach it with fear or with misapprehensions. After more than ten years spent working with active imagination, all I can say is that you could have no better or more trustworthy companion than your own unconscious. However, it is so alarmingly honest and so direct, that you will not be able to avoid having to face things you have been trying to hide. It points them out to you inexorably, but is just as ready to help you.

When you are in the early stages of the practice, certain repressions may announce themselves, so that there is a need to talk about them or even to have a good cry over them. Many Jungian analysts advise that we should make sure in advance that there will be someone available—on the phone if need be—whom we can take into our confidence when we are shaken by powerful emotions. But we must not let this discourage us: it is just as likely that after a session of active imagination the feeling will be one of having landed on a bed of roses—not of thorns!

How do we begin? Well, everyone has an individual method. The first thing to do, however, is to ensure that we are alone and that nothing and nobody will be able to disturb us. Make sure that the other members of the household understand this. Being alone was an important condition in Jung's opinion. The danger of practicing active imagination in groups is that we shall unconsciously try to produce something that will please the group or its leader, and so its naturalness will be affected. There should be no outside influence. Imagination is something you do for yourself and for no one else.

Once alone, we need to relax as completely as possible. This does not mean that we have to be stretched out at full length: but it is essential that the mind should be stilled. In any case, just stopping for a few minutes to do a little bit of imagination is utterly futile. In order to relax, we can do special exercises or can perform a certain ritual. Some people keep a special set of clothes to put on, and go to a particular place, or burn certain incense for their imagination exercises. The advantage of a ritual is that, after several repetitions of it, the ritual puts us in the right frame of mind for what we are about to do. But you might just as well go and soak in the bath or sit at your computer or word processor. It is your attitude that matters, not your position.

Provide yourself with a pen and paper for jotting down what you perceive and experience, either at the time or immediately afterward. There is no point in making notes after some time has elapsed, because the conscious will inevitably take charge and introduce, without your being aware of it, all sorts of changes. The more immediate and unadulterated your notes are, the better. Also record the date and time at which you begin.

To make a start you can take an astrological theme, but the subject does not have to be astrological. For example, you can commence with a fragment of a dream, or with some pleasant scene such as a beach or forest glade, but also with some incident in a fairy story or myth. Of course, you can simply shut your eyes and look at what appears to you. I myself have found that when I have avoided the astrological form, my choice of subject very often fits in perfectly with my current progressions and transits—something that is also true of dreams!

Naturally, for the astrological practitioner it is very interesting to see what images are evoked by the various horoscope components, whether they are planets in the signs, planets in the houses, or aspects. Don't make things too complicated to begin with. A planet in a house or in a sign usually works very well. Take any planetary position in your chart that you want to use in your imagination exercise. Look at the symbol of the planet and concentrate on it. Do not become too intense; the idea is not to let your mind wander—something the tyro is quite prone to do. Keep looking at the symbol and see what sort of images arise in connection with it, or what sounds you hear or feelings you get. Do not let the conscious mind interfere, but let what will come simply come. (Watch out that you do not fall asleep in the middle of all this delightful relaxation.) It is only natural that you will be distracted from time to time; but do not worry too much, just try to return to the matter in hand as soon as you realize what has happened.

One of two situations can occur in the image-forming. Either pictures or scenes will appear in which you play no part but feel that you are completely detached from them, or you will be personally involved in the scenes and see yourself talking and acting in them, or personified factors will converse with you. If you hold aloof, you run the risk of not having a genuine exchange with your unconscious. Certainly, you perceive the symbolic language; but, because you make no contact with it during the imagination session, its message will slip from your grasp and will sink back into the unconscious. What is very important in active imagination, is to let the pictures and scenes come naturally, and to try to build up a relationship with them, to converse with them, or to do something else with them—whatever produces an interaction between you and one or more factors in your unconscious. In short, you need to participate in the scenes, and therefore to make decisions in the scenes; you need to answer questions, and to pose your own questions too, and so on.

Now observe: the conscious is involved in your questions and other activities, but must remain completely passive with regard to the emergence of the imagery. It is free to say its own lines, but has no control over the set or over what other actors in the play are doing. So immerse yourself in the pictures you see, experience the emotions that attend them, and undergo an intense experience of what is happening in your unconscious. Everything turns on this participating, experiencing and undergoing. And do not attempt to interpret the pictures straight away; this is particularly distracting and hinders the spontaneous process. And talking of spontaneity, I must warn you that you can have experiences that will make you want to shout, cry, laugh, dance, or something of the sort. For this reason you must be somewhere where you can give free expression to these urges, uninhibited by the presence of others.

Let us take a look at an exercise in imagination to see what can happen.

A Sample Exercise

Here is a verbatim report by Atie Kaper, one of my class members, of an exercise in imagination on her Saturn in the 2nd house in Scorpio:

> I see black, stinking earth. A large cross is standing there. A huge shovel is excavating the earth. I see only the shovel and it is digging an enormously deep pit. The earth slides into the pit. It smells putrid, and the hole keeps getting bigger. "What do I have to do here?" I ask.
>
> "You must get into it," someone says.
>
> "Surely you don't expect me to get in there?" I gasp.
>
> "Of course you can," comes the reply, "If you want to go any further, you must get in."
>
> I step into the hole. It is a very long and narrow trench and I feel stifled. No matter what I do I cannot get along the trench. The whole situation becomes very emotional. Right above me, they are back-filling the trench. I feel the wet black earth hit my head with a plop. I am growing more and more frightened. I cannot go on. A voice says, "You are letting yourself be undermined, and only you can do anything about it!!!"
>
> I begin to dig with my toes like mad. Very slowly, I sink further into the ground, and more and more earth falls on my head. I work like a horse and dig and dig. The fear gradually lessens and so does the feeling of suffocation. Then, with a thud, I am in a sort of vaulted chamber. There is a great arched roof over my head. The gap through which I fell is closed again. I need to recover properly before I do anything else. My toes are dead tired; and now the feeling of suffocation has passed and I can

breathe normally. I sit and rest for a few moments. Slowly I look around me. It is not unpleasant. It feels nice. The place is dry, but there is a stream of water, and it smells good. Also there is interior lighting. I ask, "What do I have to do here?"

"Do something!" says the voice. *"Choose something!! It doesn't matter what, but do something!!"*

"Yes, but what?" I inquire. I don't know what I ought to do; I am incapable of choosing. What must I choose, anyway? I start crying and shouting desperately. I do not know which way to turn. Heavens! What shall I do? Which way shall I turn?

"Do something, Stupid! It doesn't matter what you do as long as you do something!"

I jump into the water and swim in a certain direction without a second thought. The panic attack subsides and I feel the marvelous cool water flowing over me. I feel myself getting better and begin to think I am like a fish in the water. The water is delightfully clear, and the cave becomes more and more colorful. I turn and swim splendidly. Never in my life have I felt so free; it's wonderful.

Suddenly an enormous dragon-like beast heaves itself out of the water. The monster wants to crush me or trample me to death. I am filled with fear. Then the thought flashes from my memory "You are letting yourself be undermined," so I look the dragon straight in the eye, fearlessly. Then the dragon changes into an old Indian with beautiful light blue eyes and a remarkably wrinkled face. He stands right in front of me looking at me in a friendly way. He holds my hand and I step up out of the water. Beside him is the picture of Tutankhamen. I am full of joy and I want to say something to this picture. Of course, I know that a picture cannot talk, but I have an urge to address it. The Indian says nothing; he just looks at me and lays his finger on his lips. *"Of course,"* I say, *"I talk too much."* Again, the Indian places his finger on his mouth. So we stand quietly by Tutankhamen.

Then we walk up the steps hand in hand. At the top, when I arrive there, I see an enormous light. Pure and clear. It is blinding. The light just cannot be described. It fills you completely from within. As I step into the light, I stand in a sort of desert of golden yellow warm sand. I feel the sand between my toes. The wind blows my hair and my long white dress. I feel utterly content and warm. An undescribable feeling comes over me. I felt it inside me for days.

An exercise in imagination like this should never be seen in isolation from the person to whom the imagery presents itself. Their own experiences and associations can provide much more insight into the significance of the imagination. We discussed this particular imagination in the group, and Atie added an extensive commentary. That this imagination is more than the very apt pictures of earth (the 2nd house is an earth house), and of putrefaction and stench (ascribed to Scorpio), with a large cross (which could be symbolized by both Saturn and Scorpio), will be obvious from the following account of this part of the workshop.

Karen: The 2nd house is literally the house of *terra firma*, or solid ground beneath our feet; that comes out strongly here. The stinking black earth can indicate a Scorpio theme, but equally the fear side of Saturn. The big cross tends to confirm this. Saturn is frequently depicted as the skeleton with the scythe, symbolizing death, and the cross may be another analogy of this. But the case would be materially altered if Atie has had a personal encounter with a cross. It could be a very personal symbol to her. Atie, have you had an experience in which a cross played a role?

Atie: No, definitely not.

Karen: And when I say the word "cross," what is your immediate reaction?

Atie: (at once) Death. I saw it before in a dream, in which I flew over it.

Karen: The shovel that shovels of its own accord is naturally a very surrealistic image.

Atie: (shudders and sounds horrified) Yes. And then that stinking earth: it made my flesh creep. It was also very dark, and misty and wet and clammy; I felt nauseous.

Karen: You write that a voice told you to get into this earth. What did the voice sound like?

Atie: Deep and hollow. And also very full. Full and hollow and deep. It filled the whole place, I could not escape from it. I was compelled to get in.

Karen: It was forceful then?

Atie: Yes, very forceful.

Karen: Did you associate anything with this voice?

Atie: No, absolutely not.

Karen: So it was voice out of nothing.

Atie: It sure was a spooky something. It made me gasp.

Karen: Moments like these are the ones when you need true courage in order to continue the exercise in imagination. But it is a very positive sign if you experience these emotions. People who don't experience emotion in their dreams, visualizations, and fantasies—which means that everything that comes out of their unconscious is flat and unexciting—are in real danger. Apart from that, when someone does not relate his or her feelings, we must not conclude these were absent. It may be that the person is restraining their emotions when talking about—and making associations to do with—an experience. Being scared during an imagination exercise, feeling a shiver run down the spine or, on the other hand, experiencing joy, are in themselves encouraging signs of a thorough collaboration of the unconscious in the individuation process. Anyway, then you step into the hole, which seems to have been a very narrow passage. This is a theme that often recurs in dreams and visualization, and it reminds me of the tunnel that people have seen in near-death experiences. It is also encountered in fairy tales, as in the story of the Tinder-box with its description of the narrow passage through the hollow oak. Well, you go on to say, "I feel stifled"; that is one of the forms of oppression typical of Saturn.

Atie: I was really very frightened, especially when it seemed as if they were going to back-fill the trench over me. They shoveled sand over me that fell on my head with a repeated thud. And it was done at a regular rate of working: there was a rhythm to it.

Karen: Like the steady patter of raindrops?

Atie: Precisely.

Karen: The voice that said, "You are letting yourself be undermined, and only you can do anything about it," refers, in my opinion, not only to this situation but more to an attitude to life. You consciously stepped into the "hole of problems," and had a choice of one of two things: either you could set to work under your own steam to do something about the situation, or you could let yourself be buried alive. But, if you had decided to do the latter, you would have been repeatedly made aware in daily life, during the period after the visualization, of the fact that you were letting yourself be undermined. You could repress the knowledge again, of course, but only after it has been brought to your attention. Possibly you are letting yourself be undermined out of fear of losing the solid ground under your feet (2nd house!).

Atie: I can go along with that.

Karen: What is your Sun-sign?

Atie: I am a Pisces.

Karen: You write further that you begin to dig with your toes like mad.

Atie: Yes, because I could do nothing with my arms. I was so hemmed in that the only part I could move was my toes. But I thought, I must do something. I tried everything, but felt that only my toes would work. The rest of me wouldn't move.

From group: It also makes one think of the journey through the vagina during childbirth: the vagina clasps your whole body so tightly that you cannot move a muscle.

Karen: That is possible, but here the emphasis is on the movement of the toes. Toes are very important. They are indispensable for keeping our balance in standing and walking; therefore they could symbolize some means of preserving our equilibrium. However, they could also have a personal significance. Atie, have you had a special experience to do with feet or toes?

Atie: I had an operation on my feet, on my big toe. And I have had very many dreams and imaginative experiences involving my feet. For a year now, when dreaming of a certain woman, I see my feet planted firmly on the ground, and I have the feeling that it is only in the last year that I have really enjoyed putting my feet on the ground—on the sand, with the sand running between my toes. Wonderful!

Karen: That means, of course, that this is a highly significant symbol for you personally. It may be that the fact that you have been consciously occupied with your feet in a positive sense for so long, *and* the fact that your feet are "loaded" with the operation experience, have together produced the image of you scrabbling in the earth with your feet. This image, therefore, signifies something completely different for you from what it does for the rest of us, since we have not had your experience. How did you react to the operation?

Atie: Well, not too negatively, but I have a great deal of feeling in my feet. I love it when my feet are being massaged. I relax completely then.

From group: Feet come under Pisces!

Karen: So are your feet associated with being calm and restful? And perhaps, also, with being whole?

Atie: Yes. All at once I feel a sense of restfulness rising from them.

Karen: Is it an emotional restfulness too?

Atie: Yes.

Karen: Then digging with your toes means that you are digging down to your true feeling. But you are an emotional person. So this imagination could point to a certain difficulty in encountering the outside world; and that, before doing so, you want to have firm ground beneath your feet. However, while seeking this, you run the risk of being "buried." Anyway, you started digging—how did it go?

Atie: It was suffocatingly dark. I just felt that I was sinking. Through the digging with my toes.

Karen: Yet you write that your fear gradually lessens. And then you fall into a cave. A cave usually stands for the unconscious in a general way, and for being wrapped inside a maternal embrace; but, as far as you are concerned, it could mean something quite different. Have you had any experiences with caves that made an impression on you?

Atie: No. But to some extent, caves make a disagreeable impression on me; they are so damp and clammy. I like water very much, but I don't like damp walls. The cave in my imagination was dry and really very pleasant; it felt different.

Karen: You write that the hole through which you fell was closed again.

Atie: Yes, I could no longer see where I came through. And I was completely exhausted.

Karen: In visualizations that are genuinely experienced as real events, one can physically feel this tiredness.

Atie: I agree. I felt physically exhausted.

Karen: Well now, after all your digging, you had reached a place that felt comfortable and, somehow or other, offered you protection and enclosed you—the cave. But you have not yet reached your destination. You need to do something and you don't know what it is. Seeing that the unconscious behaves like a fairy tale, and its "narrative" takes a variety of unexpected twists and turns, there is little point in making all sorts of reasoned assessments of the situation. You simply do not know what will happen next. However, you are now in a situation where you have to choose, and you say you are incapable of choosing.

Atie: I have a Libra Ascendant. . . . and I was in a bit of a panic you know. It felt okay, but I didn't have a clue what I ought to be doing there. And the voice was so strident: "Do something!" Heavens, which way should I turn?. . . . But I wanted to cope with my Saturn and I thought: "Well, I must go through with it."

Karen: Then you got into a desperate situation and began to shout and cry. This is typical of Saturn situations, in which many people get stuck as far as everyday life is concerned. They have a choice to make, but are caught in a situation that baffles them and they see no way out of it. The negative response is to sit and cry because of feelings of fear and helplessness. If you give in like this during an exercise in imagination, you will be less likely to overcome your negative reactions in ordinary life. But it is Saturn itself that spurs you on to fresh activities! Its object is not to torture people, but to prod them over barriers. It represents, as ever, our painful learning experiences. And then you jump into the water in your imagination. Water is your conscious function. It is what you could still be relying on most.

Atie: (laughs in disbelief).

Karen: Okay, but you yourself write: "I jump into the water (Water) and swim in a certain direction without a second thought (Air)." Air is your unconscious function, and as you are not exercising it by thinking, it is not operating as a jamming transmitter at this moment. And then the dragon arrives. I myself have experienced just such an imaginative episode: swimming in an underground lake in a cave, where a dragon rose up out of the water. It is an event that is often encountered in fairy tales in one form or another. But let us go on with your imagination. Your dragon threatens to crush you. First you squeezed through a narrow passage and now you are in another oppressive situation. Saturn is still at work. But you coped splendidly. Normally, the dragon is a mother symbol; and usually it comes for us in her capacity, being the mother in an archetypal sense. But it can also stand for the devouring character of the unconscious as such, and can then assume either sex. Here we see it change, because of your attitude, into a man, an old Indian, who was next to a picture of Tutankhamen. Neither the Indian nor Tutankhamen belong to Western civilization, and the unconscious often uses symbols such as these to create a certain distance. Here the male element is involved, both in the old Indian and in Tutankhamen, an Egyptian pharaoh, who died at the age of 18. A very old and a very young man are playing a part in the drama; yet both of them in a distant way. This may imply that the animus has not yet developed to the extent that is desirable for the female psyche, so that your own development potential has not been properly realized. But, before jumping to conclusions, we must examine the individual symbols. What does an Indian suggest to you? What do you associate with him?

Atie: Wisdom.

Karen: So, for you, the Indian is the symbol of the Wise Old Man?

Atie: (frankly) Yes.

Karen: What does Tutankhamen suggest to you?

Atie: He is handsome. Really handsome. Very handsome.

Karen: Thus you saw both wisdom and beauty in the shape of the Indian and Tutankhamen. But the Indian was alive and Tutankhamen was a picture. The Wise Old Man took you by the hand. It's where Saturn is so magnificent: after the painful lessons, he reaches out his hand to you, helps you on your way, and even makes you feel cheerful. What kind of hand was it?

Atie: A marvelous round, warm hand. A creative hand, but marvelous. (Becoming completely lyrical.) It was *so* lovely. To begin with it was so eerie with the dragon—and then, for something like this to happen, unbelievably ordinary. You couldn't invent anything like that.

Karen: The Indian was silent and laid his finger on his mouth several times. Your response was: "I talk too much." This could be an admonition to your unconscious element, Air, in everyday life; but Saturn is transiting the 3rd house at this time, and is letting you know in this period of your life that speech is silver, but silence is golden.

Atie: (bursts out laughing) Yes, when something emotional has happened, for example, I always have to keep on talking about it.

Karen: After this, you describe a blinding light. Your description is very reminiscent of a similar beam of white light that people who have had near-death experiences have seen; and those who have had an out-of-the-body experience also mention such a light on occasion. And the picture becomes more and more beautiful. You even experience a very intense and warm feeling, in an imagination exercise that was so dark initially and on a planet we call cold and chill—Saturn. So here we have what, for many, will be an unsuspected side of Saturn: full of toil and moil it may be, but, in the end, it has a lot of light and warmth in which one can bask—until it sets you to work again!

Atie: That fine feeling went with me. I came downstairs after the imagination exercise and my husband and children asked in amazement: "Whatever have you been doing? You seem so happy!"

Karen: Now you have been through this visualization exercise you will know, in every situation where you are metaphorically being undermined, that you are doing it yourself, and you will also know that you can escape from it yourself. What is more, that same warm feeling can return as a sort of support or help.

Further Guidance in Active Imagination

When you turn your mind's eye inward and without any preconceptions wait to see what comes, it may be that nothing at all will happen. Do not be disappointed or anxious. Sometimes the first few attempts are failures, and sometimes everything goes with a swing from the start. Perhaps you are being too eager and, without knowing it, are trying to force the pace. This is quite common in those who have turned themselves into safety mechanisms in order to keep a grip on things and let nothing get out of hand. You must become accustomed to letting everything take its course.

Possibly you will still see no pictures, even after a number of attempts. This does not matter; there are no rules about how active imagination has to take place. You can try automatic drawing, or dancing, or some other form of involuntary expression. One of these might suit your psyche better; but it is just as likely that, after a while, you will start to see imagery to which you can relate. What I advise is that you relax, choose your own procedure, and then wait to see what happens. Suppose you can exercise your imagination most easily through dancing; well, when you have finished, jot down as much as possible of the steps and evolutions you have performed. They will invariably have some symbolic meaning for you, and it is quite possible that you will really understand them in the course of time.

In individual cases there may still be a lack of success. Sometimes there is a severe blockage, but that is not always so. It may well be that the subject you wanted to use in your active imagination becomes the main theme of your dreams in the following nights by way of response.

It can also happen that images come to the surface that are so commonplace that you think nothing of them. Or, if they are a bit more arresting, you may ask yourself if they are not one of your usual fantasies. These are fairly usual reactions. But we must make one thing clear: the unconscious can express itself splendidly in the most ordinary things when you are certainly not fantasizing. Of course, you will also very often get thoughts or images of which you will say, "That is something I could never have conceived!"

Once the imagery is flowing, it often resembles a fantasy or daydream, as we have seen in the example of Saturn in Scorpio in the 2nd house. Symbols and people and also a disembodied voice appeared during the imagination exercise. Although the lady performing the excercise did not see anyone to whom the voice belonged, she did talk to it. There are several important suggestions to be made in this connection.

In the first place, when characters loom up from your unconscious, it is valuable to make contact with them. You should talk to them, and let your approach be friendly and polite. However, there is a likelihood that you will encounter factors that you had thrust aside with your conscious mind, and they will begin by behaving in an offended manner. Sometimes they will hold out for a long time and not respond (possibly during a whole series of active imagination exercises). But a friendly, polite and above all accepting attitude will eventually bring about the desired contact.

It can also happen, time after time, that as soon as you try to make active contact, the personified factor grows blurred, and approaches once more, or becomes visible again only when you do nothing and stay still. This is most likely to happen to people who are trying to rush things. It is as if their unconscious is urging them to change their behavior.

Once you have made contact with your unconscious arche-types, do let them have their say! Let them speak freely, even though that can sometimes be very unpleasant. Take them seriously, even though you do not have to swallow everything they serve up. Work out for yourself why you do not agree with them on certain points. The explanations that will occur to you will give you greater insight into everything that relates to your unconscious factors and their impact on your conscious mind.

Be completely honest with the contents of your unconscious; they will be frighteningly honest with you! If you have the courage to express your feelings to your unconscious, it will respond quite openly to this approach. If some archetype scares you, tell it so. Simply say, "You are making me afraid...." You can always ask where the entity comes from, what its intentions are, and so on. Just take care, in each case, that you do not develop any feelings of panic that would paralyze you. However, a brief panic and spasm of anxiety can occur in an imagination exercise without causing problems. If you feel a major panic attack coming on, remind your-self that the inner person or inner picture is a part of yourself. So you can always ask him or her something, and in many instances that will be all that is needed to master the panic. Questions such as, "What part of me are you?" or "Why are you giving me this feeling?" will usually improve the contact, so that the sense of panic subsides of its own accord.

Nevertheless, it can also happen that one of these inner arche-types absolutely refuses to talk, or else starts babbling a lot of gibberish of which you can make neither head nor tail. If so, follow your inclinations and see what else might work to bring about contact. For example, sing a little song to the entity, give it some-thing, make physical contact with it, dress the figure in an article of clothing, offer it food, start drawing or painting it, but do some-thing. You will observe a change gradually taking place. But what-ever you do always show respect for the being that announces itself.

Our conscious has much to learn about the unconscious. When we take the unconscious into account, many of our decisions will be considerably better balanced. On the other hand, Jung stated quite emphatically that the unconscious also has much to learn from the conscious and from our conscious attitudes. Therefore do not make yourself foolish when one of the characters from your unconscious suddenly says to you during an imagination exercise, "Go away, I don't want you now. . . ." In an active imagination exercise, you and your unconscious must be on an equal footing with one another, as Jung has repeatedly informed us. So it is very important for us to have a reasonably stable ego, one that is firm enough to resist being overpowered or carried along against its will, but one that is also flexible enough to give some space to the unconscious.

Another significant point is that we must accept *all* the responsibility for what transpires in our active imagination. If it enables you to reach a better understanding of a certain personal problem, but you try to keep on playing hide-and-seek with it in everyday life, this is tantamount to a new repression. In such a case, the unconscious can spring one or two nasty surprises on you. It is ready to help you, but is not prepared to act as a plaything for a conscious that would rather not see certain things. Nevertheless, as I have already remarked, there is no need for you to adopt everything the unconscious says. There is no need to give it your blind trust. It is the job of your conscious mind to make decisions after weighing one thing against another. You yourself must decide which advice or feelings seem to make sense, and which need to be treated with caution. If you communicate honestly with your unconscious, there will be no repercussions. In fact it is possibly on the cards that, in subsequent imagination exercises, the same archetypes will negotiate with you.

Over a limited period, active imagination sessions can differ greatly. But it is more likely that, for some time, the same archetype or personality will appear; and, quite often, you will evolve your own fairy tale or myth in which the strangest things can occur. Some series of imaginations are really publishable novels! It must be said, however, that the unconscious does not consider itself to be bound by any ethics or morals, and its contents are raw and very down-to-earth. The result is that very irrational or unethical things can happen in your visualizations. Do not try to suppress them, they belong where they are and have something to tell you. Here, too, your conscious can make an important contribution. By sharing your vision of things you can let the unconscious know what ethics and morals are. The unconscious is concerned solely with what is best for your development, without regard to the consequences for those around you. It is your conscious mind that forms the link between the desires of the unconscious and the values of the outside world. You walk a tightrope, so to speak, between these conflicting factors, and have to reach a balance with your conscious. By talking to the figures arising from the unconscious you can often help them to take a wider view. But, obviously, if you unthinkingly follow the dictates of your unconscious, you are liable to encounter the greatest difficulties in society.

Sometimes our internal factors tend to present themselves in the guise of someone we know. Actually, this image has nothing at all to do with the other person, but is purely and simply a factor within ourselves. The danger is, however, that without realizing it, we shall ascribe to this person a number of different things that do not belong to them. Consequently, what I would advise is to ask the entity to assume a different shape. In many cases this ploy succeeds. But there are other forms that can appear. Your Shadow can present itself as a person, but just as often as an animal (possibly wounded), an unkempt child, or something else that needs your care and attention. (The Shadow is always a member of your own sex.) The animal can be one you recognize; for example, a dog you once had. And the child may remind you of one of your own children, or of one belonging to a neighbor. But here again, they will depict nothing but contents in yourself, and each of them will tell you something about your unconscious.

Active imagination can be applied at various levels, of which the simplest is that, roughly speaking, we could call horse-trading, or more pedantically, "trying to reach a compromise with factors arising from one's unconscious and negotiating with them in order to be relieved of certain troubles or symptoms." Although this does bring temporary relief, it is unlikely to give satisfaction in the long-term. More thorough is the type of active imagination in which you endeavor to isolate one of your complexes or forms of behavior (something to which the planetary constellations really lend themselves) and try to understand and integrate it. This is a time-consuming process, and is not renowned for yielding quick results; although I do know of one or two small miracles. The beauty of this more leisurely process is that in all your active imagination exercises you can make friends with the characters with whom you initially crossed swords.

If you attempt to use your active imagination improperly as a tool of your ego—for example for developing paranormal powers or for strengthening the ego's other capacities, then the unconscious will turn on you sooner or later. The subtle assistance of the 12th house will be replaced by chaos and undermining! This is not to say that cosmic feelings are excluded in active imagination; on the contrary, moments can occur when everything becomes *one* and, for a brief span, you experience an ineffable form of unprecedented rest and balance. Then you are very close to the Tao, in the deepest part of the Well in the I Ching.[20] Such feelings can stay with you for a long time and can be very inspirational in all areas of your life.

As Within, So Without

Corrie Kense said in her workshop report: "I tried to visualize my Sun in the 12th house, and saw a Sun that was rather veiled. Asking the reason for this, the answer came that I was living too near my Moon and the Sun could not get through this veiling influence. I asked what I should do about it, and the reply was: "Go and paint with gold." People who are unfamiliar with these experiences suppose that one's conscious ego makes up the answers. All I can say about that is that, in this case, my ego would never have invented this solution, because I am not at all struck on gold, but much prefer silver.

I set to work painting in gold: gold suns, gold figures, and whatever came to me. This gave me a sense of excitement; I heard my heartbeat sounding in my right ear. After one or two weeks had elapsed, I began to feel uneasy with all that gold, until I became convinced that I could not go on shutting out silver. However, silver was not so easy to come by: the first shop I visited had no silver paint in stock, after that my silver paint went missing, and something happened that had never happened with the gold

---

[20]The Well or Ching is hexagram 48 of the I Ching. Tr.

paint, I twice placed my hand on the silver paint when it was still wet.

And while I was painting in gold I was confronted with other gold items: at a bus stop a young man stood beside me who took a tube of gold paint out of a bag, and a few days later I found a gold-colored bracelet at another bus stop. Suddenly it occurred to me that even before the visualization I had unconsciously occupied myself with gold: I had a Denderah Zodiac painted on papyrus in two shades of gold, and had also purchased a poster with a gold-colored picture on it. The latter I had hung over my bed."

So what happened in Corrie's case? She listened to her unconscious, set to work with gold paint, and even came across it at the bus stop. It is certainly not an everyday occurrence for someone to take a tube of gold paint out of a bag while standing next to you waiting for a bus. Jung would have called this a splendid example of synchronicity. You encounter in the outer world the very thing with which you are preoccupied. Painting with gold also produced definite emotions, always a sign that something that needs to be released is being released. When, feeling the need for balance (she is a Libra) Corrie also wanted to use silver paint, her unconscious gave her to understand in no uncertain terms that the time was not yet ripe: not only did she smudge it twice (which had never happened with the gold paint!) but she met with resistance in the outside world. First there was no silver paint for sale, and second she herself (unconsciously) mislaid it when she had it.

Through the answer of the unconscious that she should start working in gold paint, she realized some time later that, without being aware of it, she had already been occupied with the theme of gold, seeing the poster and the papyrus were both richly colored with gold paint. It was therefore the right time for that theme. For a conscious mind that is absorbed in the material world, the whole thing will seem somewhat bizarre: you see a veiled sun and hear out of nowhere a voice telling you that you must paint in gold. What on earth is the sense in that? A year after her experience, I asked Corrie what it had released in her and if she had undergone a permanent change. "The whole process gave me a sense of liberation," was her reply. "That sense has not deserted me. Also I am much more prepared to stand up for myself in an unruffled way. This is what has been released in me."

As we have seen, Corrie encountered things in the outside world that were totally in agreement with what was going on inside her. The effect was actually very concrete. The relationship between the inner and outer worlds is much stronger than we generally recognize; something that Carl Jung stressed. The more responsive you are to the unconscious, the more successfully you will grasp and understand the interplay between signals from the outside world and your inner symbolism, without having to fall into any kind of superstition. What you have then is a living exchange between your conscious and your unconscious, followed by a living exchange between the world inside you and the world outside you!

Carl Jung used to say to his students and coworkers: "Never conduct a workshop on active imagination without telling the story of the Chinese rain-maker of Kiau Tchou." This is a true story that Jung had heard first hand from his friend, the sinologue Richard Wilhelm, one of the best-known translators of the I Ching. The story runs as follows:

"A terrible drought was devastating the part of China where Richard Wilhelm lived. The inhabitants had done everything in their power to get rain, but nothing did any good. Finally they decided to call in a rain-maker. This interested Wilhelm enormously, and he made sure he was present when the rain-maker arrived. The man came in a covered wagon. He was a little wizened old man who, as soon as he had stepped down from the wagon, sniffed the air with obvious dislike. He asked to be left alone for a few days in a small hut on the edge of town. His meals were to be left outside the door.

"For three days nothing was heard of him; and then it began not only to rain but also to snow heavily—which was something that had never happened before at that time of year. Deeply impressed, Wilhelm sought out the rain-maker and asked him how he could make rain and even snow. The rain-maker simply said, "I did not make the snow. I am not responsible for it." But Wilhelm pressed the matter and reminded him that they had been suffering from a dreadful drought until he came, and that three days after his arrival they had actually had enormous quantities of snow. The old man answered, "Oh, I can explain that. I come from a place where people are in balance; they are in Tao, and so the weather is also in order. But, as soon as I got here, I saw that the people were out of balance, and they infected me. And so I remained alone until I was in Tao once more, and then of course it began to snow."

In the same vein, Barbara Hannah quotes the tale of Saint Gertrude. It was said of this Benedictine Mother Superior that she was able to end a hard frost. It was also well known that people were healed in answer to her prayers. Accounts of her prayers reveal something very significant, namely that she made absolutely no attempt to impose her ego or her will on God. All she did was to pray that He would give His attention to her request. After that, she endeavored to be in full harmony with Him. And even if nothing happened, she was determined that it would not alter her feelings toward God. Being in complete unity with Him, without needing to see results earns its just reward!

You can think of God in terms of Tao, and in a certain sense you can see Him reflected in the Jungian concept of the Self. For our present purposes, it does not matter much what concept or religious viewpoint you choose as long as you learn to live with an attitude in which the ego remains completely intact as the center of consciousness and is free to develop, and yet can step back a little in order to make room for the world of the unseen and indefinable which is, astrologically speaking, the world of the 12th house.

In the 12th house lies the Great Union with nature inside us and outside us. There is no other factor in the horoscope that brings us so close to the source of the life-stream, as does the so often misunderstood 12th house.

11

The Story
of
Gerard Croiset

An Example

One of The Netherland's most renowned psychics is the late Gerard Croiset, a gifted clairvoyant who was continually prepared to collaborate in scientific research on the paranormal. Much has been written about him, and he also wrote his autobiography. We therefore have the opportunity to look at the events in his life and also see how he himself experienced them. The latter is important, because a natal chart is more apt to show how one experiences life, or how one is likely to react to things, rather than presenting the happenings of life as objective facts. By studying his life's events and what he felt about them, we shall hope to ascertain what role the 12th house played.

Gerard Croiset was born on the 10th of March, 1909, prematurely. He was physically weak, and a few days after birth he was virtually dehydrated by enteritis. No one thought he would survive; but he recovered, as he always did on later occasions in life. The Croisets were very poor and, throughout his youth, Gerard was confronted by the most varied problems. Also other circumstances into which he was born were unusual. His father, Hijman

Croiset, married to Judith Boekbinder, was an idealist at heart who found it rather difficult to cope with everyday life. He was interested in the future, and was never afraid to make drastic changes in his lifestyle when to do so was more in line with his ideals. He had little thought for what this might do to his family. Croiset called his parents progressive and eccentric. They lived and dressed according to their own lights, and went their own way.

His parents enlisted in the movement started by Frederik van Eeden, and became keen advocates of an alternative community inspired by socialism. This meant openly living and working with the members of a commune under the motto: "All for one, and one for all." The basis was purely idealistic, which suited Croiset's father perfectly.

The commune was a haven of free love, and Croiset writes that this created problems, not least because people joined the commune with the main idea of gratifying their sexual appetites without restraint. Therefore Gerard's parents left the commune and decided to have a normal wedding, though with no intention of abandoning their ideals. The marriage, however, did not last and his parents separated. From the age of 7, Gerard was for the most part brought up by others: first of all by his maternal grandmother, and then temporarily in a children's home before living with various foster families, and so on.

Croiset provides more information about his father. Although the latter detested contemporary society because it had a long way to go before matching his ideals, he did enjoy life to the full. He seems to have had a constant fear of death, and the smallest pimple would start him worrying about blood poisoning. This obsession gave him a fancy for playing the doctor, and he would even advise others on their health. As it happens, he seems to have displayed flashes of paranormal insight into medical matters, but he refused to admit this. In fact, he denied most vehemently that there was anything unusual going on. He was scared of the supernatural and scared of dying. Croiset writes, "He strove to uncover the secret of life in order to be able to manage it at will. This made death seem less inevitable to him. Yet in his inmost soul he was afraid that death would overtake him before he had realized his ideals. This caused him to try and experience far too quickly everything there was to experience. Or, to put it another way, he was always thirsting to attain the unattainable. And so he hotted up the pace in order to try out a number of methods for living life as intensely as possible. He became possessed by an overstrung and distorted philosophy of life, and became more and more of a dissident."

His 12th House

Gerard Croiset's life had a troubled start, and was no bed of roses at any time while he was growing up. Let us see what the 12th house has to say. See chart 7.

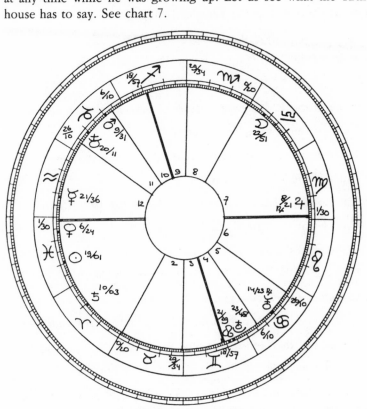

Chart 7. Natal chart of Gerard Croiset, born March 10, 1909, Laren, Holland, at 6:00 A.M.

We see one planet in the 12th, namely Mercury. This planet rules two houses: the 4th (with Gemini on the cusp) and the 7th (with Virgo on the Descendant). The 12th house itself has two rulers: Saturn, because Capricorn is on its cusp, and Uranus, because Aquarius is intercepted in the 12th house. We shall have to consider the position of these two rulers when we come to make our analysis. All told, there are the following components that comprise Croiset's twelfth-house situation:

- Mercury in the 12th

- Ruler of the 4th in the 12th

- Ruler of the 7th in the 12th

- Ruler of the 12th (Saturn) in the 1st

- Ruler of the 12th square Mars

- Ruler of the 12th square co-ruler of the 1st (Mars)

- Ruler of the 12th square Neptune

- Ruler of the 12th square the ruler of the 1st (Neptune)

- Ruler of the 12th inconjunct Jupiter

- Ruler of the 12th inconjunct the ruler of the 10th (Jupiter)

- Co-ruler of the 12th (Uranus) in the 11th

- Co-ruler of the 12th square the Moon

- Co-ruler of the 12th square ruler of the 5th (Moon)

- Co-ruler of the 12th opposite Neptune

- Co-ruler of the 12th opposite the ruler of the 1st (Neptune)

- Co-ruler of the 12th sextile Sun

- Co-ruler of the 12th sextile co-ruler of the 6th (Sun)

Obviously there are many factors tied in with the 12th house. Let's see how we can interpret them and what traces of them we can find in the life and experience of Gerard Croiset.

First of all, we see Mercury in the 12th. As we know from earlier chapters, various matters can be represented by the 12th:

the situation attending the birth, the experiences of the child in its mythic phase, possible problems and repressions of the parents and/or their hidden gifts and talents; and all these can be connected with specific family problems. We must remember these points when interpreting each 12th-house factor.

Mercury is the planet of contact and communication, of writing, talking, thinking, analyzing and connecting, to name but a few of the things it governs. In some people with Mercury in the 12th (or in aspect to the ruler of the 12th) there seems to have been problems with contacts in the earliest stage of life. For example: one or both parents may fail to respond to the signals from the young child, or may give it insufficient attention; the parent or parents may never or hardly ever talk to it, giving it too little mental stimulus or leaving it alone for long periods in a situation where there is not enough going on. The same applies to the toddler, who is also liable to get too little contact or verbal stimulus.

This may certainly have played a part in the case of Croiset. We have already seen how his father sailed through everyday life with his thoughts continually fixed on the future. In such circumstances the attention needed by the child can go by the board. Croiset himself relates the following incident. He once spent three consecutive days trying to saw through a branch with a toy saw. He began to feel that the task was too much for him but eventually managed it. Triumphantly, he showed the two pieces to his father, who had just become involved in a political argument with a visitor and displayed no interest in the victory of his 6-year-old son. "My achievements were never important to *him*," writes Croiset. When Croiset once complained to his father about this, his parent's reaction was: "Why do you always have to have so much attention?"

Of course, a single incident like this need not imply that his father persistently failed to take any notice of him; but, when someone remembers and attaches importance to an event like this, it must have made a deep impression. It is felt deeply, and that is what we find in the chart. What is more, it emerges from the biography as a whole that the father had attached extremely little importance to his upbringing; so it is highly likely that this example illustrates the usual behavior of the father toward the son.

In addition, I have often seen Mercury in the 12th have a very different effect in families where the child did receive a lot of attention. What happens then is that the child gives very unclear signals (or, in general, none at all), so that it is not understood, or heard when it should be heard. In that case, even when the parents have the best intentions, the child can feel misunderstood and insecure. I can think of a baby that would lie quietly without uttering a sound, and looking contented even though it was wearing a dirty diaper, which must have been especially irritating because it was already suffering from nappy rash. The parents simply did not know when the baby's diapers needed changing and when it did not.

I have encountered this position, too, in the charts of children one of whose parents had academic leanings but had never had the chance to satisfy them, or had shown promise as a writer but had never developed the talent. Be that as it may, the placement is one in which open and direct communication becomes a weak point. On the other hand, it can help the native to follow other types of communication and to learn to react to unconscious communication. Therefore this placement can contribute to paranormal abilities, even though the individual may be disinclined to develop them initially. The uncertainty surrounding communication, contacts and thinking that the young person with Mercury in the 12th usually experiences, can find expression in a continual craving for attention and in bothering other people with questions and remarks. Perhaps the reply, "Why do you always have to have so much attention?" wrung out of Croiset's father, may have had something to do with this. Other forms of expression arising from this uncertainty can be building a private fantasy and thought world, and possibly writing poetry, keeping diaries, solving puzzles, etc.

Mercury is also ruler of the 4th and ruler of the 7th. Quite often I have met a connection between the 4th and the 12th house in those who have had a rather chaotic youth, generally with little emotional security. Sometimes such people have for years had the feeling that they were not living with their real parents, that they did not belong to the family in which they grew up; or they do not feel that they belong anywhere, or they do not feel capable of settling down anywhere, or they are not sure about their true background. Unspoken questions about family life also quite often crop up with this placement. In positive cases, however, there was a wonderful atmosphere in the home, often with plenty of music-making or other artistic pursuits, mutual understanding, or a situation in which religion or the church was a factor holding the family together. Unfortunately the positive expressions of the ruler of the 4th in the 12th are few and far between in my experience. In most instances, this placement is associated with a sense of alienation in some form or other.

The experiences of Gerard Croiset are characteristic for his chart. Alienation was part of his life from birth. His parents were unable to create peace and security in the family environment.

Another illustration is the instance of a woman who took part in my 12th-house workshops. In analyzing the 12th houses of her family, we found that her father and mother had no links between the 12th house and the 4th house. But all seven children had a 12th/4th house connection, as did four of the six grandchildren. In the radix, the father has Pluto in the 4th house, and the mother a void of course Moon. Pluto in the 4th is often associated with an emotional sensitivity that leads the individual to hide or deny his or her feelings. Something is going on under the surface, but not for others to see. There can also be a flight into sharp behavior with an underlying note of fear and insecurity. Only after this fear has been faced, can a solid emotional basis be formed, but this takes time.

An unaspected Moon may well mean for the mother that, for a long while, she wondered whether she was a good mother or not. Often this is a tormenting question, which is overcompensated by tender behavior alternating with a failure to cuddle the child when it really needs comforting. The giving of warmth and loving care is initially not easy to do. Over-reacting and also a failure to react is involuntary more often than not. Here, too, we see that a gradual process of confrontation with the above-mentioned fear *and* the gradual discovery that everything goes well as long as no one expects anything of the individual, can give a more tranquil attitude. With increased confidence, such an unaspected Moon can produce the sort of caring that is cheerful and even-tempered, with less capriciousness. The insecurity, however, can carry over into adult life. To sum up, the situation arising is one of the conflicts concerning giving care and attention in the family. This is expressed in the natal charts of both parents, though in a different manner. The struggle with this conflict in a positive sense and the repressions and overcompensation involved in a negative sense, may have left their mark on the children, all of whom have links between the 12th and the 4th house. The conflict can follow through in succeeding generations, who may well inherit the same pattern. This is often seen (with varying combinations) when one studies the horoscopes of several generations of the same family.

In a positive sense, such a connection between the 12th and the 4th house betokens perhaps that you let the emotional basis and desire to care for others associated with the 4th house combine with the empathy natural to the 12th. Out of sympathy and compassion, you interest yourself in the difficult circumstances of people and animals and offer to help and care for them. This is one of the constructive possibilities. Emotional insecurity and difficulty in finding a settled atmosphere to enjoy are negative aspects of the placement, and there is a great need of tenderness to aggravate the situation. Nevertheless, the conflict or dilemma can be overcome very successfully in the long run.

The ruler of the 7th in the 12th in Croiset's chart could have something to do with the fact that, because of his experiences, he was not easily able to form a balanced, ordinary social picture of how a relationship or a marriage should be (7th house). This may have affected his thinking and may have led him, for example, to idealize too much. Which brings us automatically to the possibility that, through this connection between the 12th and the 7th house, Croiset could have been naturally very receptive toward the idealistic and idealizing element in his parents' marriage without reference to the question of how much of the idealism really shone through in their relationship. It is very difficult to determine what took precedence; the experience of a certain situation, or the interpretation of events in keeping with character traits that were present at birth (see also chapter 5).

In itself, the presence of the ruler of the 7th house in the 12th house need not imply that the parents' marriage was bad, or that they were always drunk; although cases are sometimes encountered in which, during the child's early years, the parents passed through difficult or undermining situations, as happened to Croiset's parents when their commune ideal was spoiled. Once or twice I have come across cases in which there were great changes in the relationship between the parents in the period when the child who had a 12th/7th house connection was still small. The changes usually had to do with an increased sensitivity toward one another—even an almost telepathic contact—or with an improvement in the relationship through the agency of music, art, yoga, meditation, hypnosis, imagination, religion and the like.

The ruler of the 12th in the 1st also contributed to Croiset's sensitivity. Again and again I encounter connections between the 12th and the 1st house in those who are extremely sensitive to feelings and atmospheres, who have imperceptibly reacted to them from an early age. Often, without being aware of it, these people absorb the tensions in their surroundings or, at least, are influenced by them. For example, they can share someone's headache, or can undergo an involuntary mood-change apparently without any assignable cause, or suddenly feel sorrowful or unable to concentrate, or are tense and nervous. It is quite possible that their over-sensitivity will make them exhausted or ill. Often they fail to realize that the headache, change of mood, sadness or strain, have originated in someone else and that they have unintentionally tuned into it. Gradually they will come to realize that this is so.

Frequently this causes further problems. If you often feel a sudden change inside you, and if this makes you feel uneasy or uncomfortable, this in itself can be distressful. It is natural to think that you are not being accepted by the outside world, and this impression may be strengthened by all sorts of things. For example, when you walk into a room where two people have just been having words with one another but are now putting on a show of sweet reasonableness. The atmosphere of the quarrel will still hang heavily in the air, and if you have a connection between the 12th and the 1st house, you will inevitably sense it. What is crucial is how you interpret the disagreeable atmosphere. If you do not know how sensitive you are (and certainly, as a child, you will not know it), the perception of such a tense atmosphere is enough to create the idea that the individuals in the room do not like you, want nothing to do with you, and are just being nice for the sake of good manners. This can make you creep into your shell and just hide away. The two individuals who had been quarrelling, in their turn, do not know why you are so reserved or why you do not get in touch with them again for such a long time. Incomprehension and misunderstandings in relationships with the outside world   entirely possible with such a combination.

Children born with this type of chart are not adept at dealing with those around them. This seems to also have been a problem shared by one of the parents or grandparents. On the other hand, this type of sensitivity can make a significant contribution to the development of paranormal abilities. In our example chart, Croiset has many ties between the 12th house and the 1st: the ruler of the 12th in the 1st, the ruler of the 12th square the ruler of the 1st and square the co-ruler of the 1st, and the co-ruler of the 12th in opposition to the ruler of the 1st. To judge by these chart factors, it is more than likely that he was unusually sensitive in all his early contacts with the outside world. Such sensitivity can have a physical effect. Consider Croiset's frail state of health.

With the ruler of the 12th square Mars, there often appears to have been suppressed aggression in the parents and/or grand-parents, a certain fear of quarrels and violence, an unwillingness to stand up for themselves and to say "I" with determination. As we saw in earlier chapters, these repressions and fears are generally overcompensated for by an over-eagerness to be at everyone's beck and call in order to serve them more or less obtrusively. I have met this form of expression in an extreme and in a milder form when Mars is in the 12th or in aspect to the ruler of the 12th. With this placement, it is easier to stand up for others than to fight one's own battles. Great satisfaction can be obtained by self-dedication to a collective goal, by espousing the cause of minorities or of the disadvantaged, or by crusading for animal rights.

Croiset expressed all that in his own manner. He was both a psychic and a paranormal healer, and he helped many people for little or no financial reward. But when people took advantage of his good nature, by putting a button in the contribution box instead of money for example, he had great difficulty in taking them to task. In fact he used to get quite upset about it, from sheer frustration. It is something I see quite often with Mars in the 12th or aspecting the ruler of the 12th: these people are shy of asking favors for themselves; only when they are on their own do they give vent to anger and vexation. The anger is usually held in check and simply shows as fits of grumpiness from time to time.

It is not entirely clear whether or not the difficulty experienced by Croiset in standing up for himself had been shared by this parents or grandparents. Nothing is said about this in his autobiography or in articles about him. His father does not seem to have suffered from this problem, seeing that he went his own provocative way and displayed considerable pluck on a number of occasions. I get the impression, however, from Croiset's writings that his mother may have been more self-sacrificing than she really wanted to be. She was left to look after the children on her own. After the divorce she worked day and night to support them. But the strain was too much for her and she ended up in hospital. Later on she married a much older man, who had been a bachelor until he was 62. The lack of understanding between him and the children was so bad, that Gerard Croiset was again taken into care by a foster-family. Although we must not put everything down to it, it does seem as if the problems represented by the ruler of the 12th square Mars in Croiset's horoscope flowed from certain problems belonging to his mother.

The ruler of the 12th square Neptune and the co-ruler of the 12th in opposition to Neptune are further important indications of Croiset's sensitivity. I very often meet with links between the 12th house and Neptune in children of families that harbor paranormal gifts but, in many cases, without doing much or indeed anything to cultivate them. I have known cases in which one of the parents discovered that he or she possessed paranormal abilities only after the child had discovered similar abilities! But in the case of Croiset, he writes that, on a number of occasions, his father gave evidence of paranormal gifts, but wanted nothing to do with them. In the father they were present but suppressed; in the son, we have Neptune in aspect to the ruler of the 12th (and to the co-ruler of the 12th). Such a connection between Neptune and the 12th house need not always signify paranormal abilities. I have also encountered latent artistry, musicality, sensitivity to symbolism and dreams, a liking for day-dreaming, healing powers and the like.

Another possibility that I have encountered fairly often in a connection between Neptune and the 12th house is that of parents who come from different religious backgrounds (something I have also observed when Jupiter is linked with the 12th). Often, with this position, the individual develops a personal religious outlook, which is not necessarily bound up with organized religion, but comes from within and is felt and experienced in the inner depths of being. Idealism and a self-sacrificing nature are frequently part of the picture, combined with quick sympathies and a desire to help others. I cannot throw off the impression that Croiset's father felt even less at home with idealism than he did with his paranormal gifts. Otherwise, would he have needed to chase after his ideals so desperately, even at the expense of his family, and would the results have been so drastic? I believe that it is quite possible that the ruler of the 12th square Neptune, and the co-ruler of the 12th in opposition to Neptune, relate to the unbalanced idealism of Croiset's two parents, but especially with that of his father, which produced such havoc in his life.

The inconjunct between the ruler of the 12th and Jupiter contributes something further. Jupiter is the planet of expansion, of widening one's horizons, of broadening one's range of interests. It treats the unattainable as attainable and, with its sweeping vision, can perform wonders. But there are obvious problems with this, and the problem side of Jupiter is seen in the elder Croiset, since we find Gerard writing, "He was always desperately trying to reach what was out of reach." The fact that this was due partly to the fear of death that haunted Croiset's father is neither here nor there. Croiset was sensitive to the desire for unfettered expansion that affected his father, and admitted that he himself was always inclined to aim too high.

The fact that the aspect is an inconjunct may have contributed to the general feeling of unrest. But the most important fact is that there is an aspect at all: its type does not alter the core meaning. Croiset also says that his father quite enjoyed playing the doctor. As it happens, I have more than once encountered Jupiter in the 12th or in aspect to the ruler of the 12th in the charts of children who have one parent who wanted to be a doctor or teacher, or who dreamed of traveling or studying, but had never had the chance. Many of these parents had long ago repressed their youthful ambitions, but were unaware that their dream-wishes had manifested in the next generation, although in a veiled form supplied by the obscure 12th house. Physicians are benefited by this placement or aspect, as it enables them to communicate with and to obtain information from their patients by indirect means; they may not be able to give a rational account of how they formed their diagnosis in every instance, but the help they indirectly receive is very valuable. The operation of a "sixth sense" certainly seems to have entered into Gerard Croiset's healing work.

The aspects of Jupiter and Neptune with the two rulers of the 12th house could also represent a deep-rooted need to experience a unity with every living thing; an almost religious experience of the union of men and women with humanity as a whole and with nature. They could also represent the search for a synthesis of things, and the gaining of a vision in which this synthesis stands in the foreground. Therefore these aspects are very favorable for a religious vocation, for work on behalf of the third world, for activities in defense of animals, children, human rights, etc., and for championing the rights of underprivileged groups or of those living on the fringe of society (minorities, addicts). They are also very helpful for spiritual work, alternative medicine, alternative lifestyles and the like. The dangers are excessive idealism in which self and/ or reality is lost to sight, chasing after an unattainable ideal, following (or even being) a false prophet, and so on. Where the 12th house is concerned, we must never forget that we are on the edge of the collective unconscious, which threatens to swallow up anything connected with the house. Planets in the 12th or in aspect to the ruler of the 12th show where we run the risk of being swallowed up by the collective unconscious, but also how we can tap this deep source. Therefore the house is one where we have to maintain a perpetual balance on the dividing line between the personal and the collective.

The ruler of the 12th is square the ruler of the 5th. Traditionally, the 5th house stands for hobbies, sport, gambling and pleasure. Self-confidence and children are also found there, however, it is constantly being shown to me that the meaning of the 5th house goes deeper than this. It is not so much the external child that we find in this house as the child in ourselves—in other words, the degree of openness, anticipation and self-reliance with which we dare to encounter life. I think it also shows how much we are prepared to enjoy the things that come to us, just as a child can have an immediate enjoyment of what it has been offered. Allowing oneself to enjoy things and expressing the pleasure they give are very 5th-house qualities that are most important for a feeling of well-being and of feeling free to express oneself. The stronger this feeling is in us, the easier it is to pass on to our children. In this respect, we do encounter our own physical children in the 5th house—in the form of our attitude to them as a consequence of our attitude toward the child in ourselves. By giving ourselves, without restraint, the space to indulge in all sorts of hobbies and activities, simply for the fun of it, we encourage and stimulate our children to explore the world.

If there is a connection between the 12th house and the 5th house, there are, by and large, two ways in which it can express itself. If we seal up the 12th house out of fear of what we might find deep inside it, we transport the chaos and uncertainty of that house into the 5th house. Among other things, this can lead to uncertainty over what we find entertaining, a lack of self-confidence, and a dependent and questing attitude. If we are prepared to admit our sensitivity, however, the connection between the two houses can signify many activities and hobbies that are somehow associated with the contents of the 12th house; examples are an interest in dreams, mythology, fairy stories and legends, hypnosis, meditation and religion, and also in the "ocean" of the universe. In addition, music or art, involvement in the paranormal and, of course, drink, drugs and other forms of addiction, belong to the 12th house. A connection with the 5th house can mean a special interest in such things; for example, someone becomes a wine buff or a student of the history or action of drugs. The sort of hobby more particularly associated with a 5th-house/12th house connection is the one you pursue in peace and quiet on your own.

Thus, it is certainly not true that the connection between the two houses will lead to a chaotic situation or, at the very least, to an identity crisis. But since the negative side of the connection predominated in the case of Croiset, matters were decidedly difficult one would think. As we have already seen, with Mars in the 12th house, he found it hard to stand up for himself. A problem-oriented 12th/5th-house connection also goes hand-in-hand with a lack of self-assertion in the sense that the individual hesitates to let people see who he or she is and what he or she wants.

The life of Gerard Croiset shows us that he did not suppress his sensitivity, in spite of the fact that he did not receive much understanding in the early part of his life. In his case there is a merging of the 12th and 5th houses with the 6th; and so his deepest

interest and his hobby—the area of the paranormal and of healing—
became his work.

This brings us to the following connection with Croiset's 12th
house: co-ruler of the 12th square the ruler of the 6th and co-ruler
of the 12th sextile the co-ruler of the 6th. Here are two connections
between the 6th and the 12th house: one of them harmonious and
the other one disharmonious. The fact that there is more than one
connection is enough in itself to make this combination significant.
The sextile between the co-ruler of the 12th and the co-ruler of
the 6th can help to alleviate the strain of the square between the
co-ruler of the 12th and the ruler of the 6th. The connection shows
that 12th-house factors are trying to be expressed in the broadest
possible sense in the area of work, sickness and health. In my
experience, this connection seems to work out very nicely even
when the aspect is hard, provided the individual is prepared to use
his or her sensitivity and sixth sense. If the development is well-
balanced, it can give a social conscience, a good nose for future
trends in one's line of work and an ability to find solutions for
problems that seem to be insoluble. A prerequisite is a willingness
to relax and to rely on that inscrutable inner "something." Also,
with this aspect, there can be a genuine (not assumed or hypocrit-
ical) religious input into work and the everyday life situation.

Quite often we find that operating with invisible energies forms
part of the work—for example, in the preparation of homeopathic
remedies or applying them medically, or carrying out research into
things of this sort that still defy explanation. Traditionally, the feet
are governed by the 12th house; and, indeed, people such as re-
flexologists, podiatrists, or manufacturers of special orthopedic
footwear, who are professionally involved with the feet, generally
seem to have a prominent 12th house, and more often than not a
connection between houses 12 and 6. Anyway, as we have already
seen, Croiset was a psychic and a paranormal healer, and worked
in this manner with invisible energies.

However, in those who shut their eyes to the depths of the
12th house and dare not face the world of the irrational, a connection between the 6th and the 12th house has different impli-
cations. Thus I have encountered attitudes toward work varying
from one extreme where one person says, "I am only a drudge,"
through the other extreme where he or she says, "I don't work,

because if I did I should lose my mystical gifts." This connection can also be present in diseases that prove impossible to diagnose, or in all sorts of vague complaints and the like.

Croiset has the co-ruler of the 12th sextile the Sun and square the Moon. In chapter 6, I have given a detailed account of the possible effects of a connection between the 12th house and the Sun and Moon, and it might be a good idea for the reader to refer again now to what was said there. The connection of the two lights, the Sun and Moon, with the 12th house increases Croiset's sensitivity and empathy. The influence of the connection with the Sun is easily traced in what Croiset said about his father neglecting the family because of the pressure of other things. The conflict with the Moon need not mean that his mother failed him. It could signify that one of his parents was very impressionable or easily hurt. Possibly the problems encountered in the commune by the parents during Croiset's first years of life, and the lack of sincerity there, are represented in the link between the Moon and the 12th house. There is also the possibility that one of the parents (the mother?) found the course of events very hard to handle, or was busy trying to assimilate past emotional experiences. We can do no more than make a guess at the latter.

Where there is a connection between the Sun or the Moon and the 12th house, a question mark sometimes hangs over the child's health. In Croiset's case, health does seem to have been a problem; however, the trouble is just as likely to be a certain separation, real or emotional, between parent and child. It is impossible to judge the extent to which the link between Sun and Moon and Croiset's 12th house was inherited from either of his parents, because we do not have their horoscopes.

It goes without saying that our parents have a great influence on our eventual outlook on life. In the 10th house lies the picture we form of ourselves and the way society sees us. The 10th house is also to some extent colored by the parental influence: the 4th/10th-house axis is always the axis that has to do with our encounter with our parents (see chapter 6). Croiset had the ruler of the 12th inconjunct the ruler of the 10th, which indicates that the idea he had of himself was colored by the 12th house. Incidentally, I have often noticed that when the parents work and live on what are called the fringes of society (and I do not mean this disparagingly), the children quite frequently have the following: Neptune or ruler of 12th house in the 10th house, or in aspect to the MC or to the ruler of the 10th. When I talk of fringe activities, I am taking the broad view. The world of art and music, in which there are breaks between exhibitions or gigs, and an air of glamor or romance, are examples of what I mean; as are activities in the alternative field—alternative medicine, astrology, hypnotherapy and faith healing. But there can also be a negative side. I have found these positions in a child of two junkies, and in a child whose father was an alcoholic.

The 12th house tends to blur out 10th-house identity, and to leave us without a clearcut self-image. Many people with this combination are unsure of what attitude they should adopt. Some of them allow their opinion of themselves to be decided by what other people think—which only makes them more confused. However, it is also true that if the people develop the courage to defend the irrational, sensitive side of the 12th house, they acquire a completely stable form of confidence—without being able to explain it in words. An identity is formed in which empathy and intuition are important, and presentiments play a significant part. For example, a nurse with such a placement or aspect can, if open to its influence, often feel impelled, without knowing why, to enter such and such a ward at a timely moment when help is urgently required. One could almost say there was something like a radio link with crisis points. But the channel to the unconscious mind must be kept tuned in, otherwise the same placement or aspect will probably produce uncertainty and chaotic situations. For those who can approach their work with sufficient sensitivity, the placement is a fine one in principle. Certainly, Croiset seems to have profited hugely from it.

Finally, we come to the fact that Croiset's co-ruler of the 12th was in the 11th. This gave the need to have an idealistic circle of friends with whom he could enjoy an unspoken understanding. The danger of this is that one's ideals can be determined by what is approved by the circle; yet, if one's development is balanced, an outlet for one's inner motives and ideals can be found in others. But, if the 12th house influence is denied expression, then with a ruler (or co-ruler) of the 12th in the 11th, the chaotic components in the circle of friends can come to the fore. On the other hand, if an open attitude is preserved toward 12th-house matters, this can impart a deep sense of trust to very fine, and often spiritual, friendships. In a fair number of cases, I have seen people with such a placement look for friends with whom they could discuss spiritual and religious topics, or talk about symbols and dreams, or parapsychology, or on any other wide-ranging subject. Music-making with others is a further possible mode of expression. In his earlier period, Croiset conducted a number of spiritistic experiments with friends and acquaintances. When this fell more into the background, his contacts with those he called his spiritual friends became more intense. Also his friendship with a Calvinistic teacher, Dick Wieringa, was very important to him. He had many conversations with him, and he writes that this man, who knew the Bible by heart, had a big influence on his thought-world.

Late contacts also belong to the sphere of the co-ruler of the 12th in the 11th. Worth mentioning is the prolonged contact with Prof. W.H.C. Tenhaeff, freemason and parapsychologist. They carried out numerous parapsychological tests together.

The life of Gerard Croiset is a beautiful illustration of both the problems and the brighter side of the 12th house. Much of what we read in his autobiography confirms my own experiences with the 12th house. Life provides an endless variety of situations and possible forms of expression of astrological factors; therefore our study of Croiset's 12th house can do no more than serve as an example, as a means of gaining some insight into the way in which things can work out and interweave, and as an encouragement to the reader to study the matter further. Croiset called himself a happy man. Well, we all have a potential for happiness, although it sometimes seems out of reach. Certainly, it will never be found in the 12th house . . .

Bibliography

Ammann, A. N. *Aktive Imagination: Darstellung einer Methode.* Olten, 1978.

Atkinson, R. I., R. C. Atkinson & E. R. Hilgard. *Introduction to Psychology.* New York: Harcourt Brace Jovanovich, 1983.

Birkauser-Oeri, S. *Die Mutter in Märchen: Deutung der Problematik das Muttlischen und des Mutterkomplexsus am Beispiel bekannter Märchen.* Stuttgart, 1978.

Buck, P. *East Wind, West Wind.* New York: John Day Books, 1973.

Croiset, G. *Croiset paragnost.* Naarden, 1978.

Damen, T. *Oosprong en vervulling. Astrologische symboliek in mandala's.* Nijmegen, 1987.

Dieckmann, H. *Träume als Sprache der Seele. Einfurhrung in die Tramdeutung der Analytischen Psychologie C.G. Jungs.* Fellbach, 1978.

Edelstien, M. G. *Trauma, Trance & Transformation: A Clinical Guide to Hypnotherapy.* New York: Brunner-Mazel, 1981.

Ehrenwald, J. *The ESP Experience: A Psychiatric Validation.* Convention of the Parapsychological Assn., New York, 1978.

Eisenbud, J. *Parapsychology and the Unconscious.* Berkeley: North Atlantic, 1983.

Fordham, M. "The Life of Childhood," *Analytical Psychology*. London, 1947.

Fraiberg, S. H. *The Magic Years: Understanding and Handling the Problems of Early Childhood*. New York: Scribner, 1984.

Franz, M. L. von. *Individuation in Fairy Tales*. Dallas: Spring Publications, 1977.

——. *Problems of the Feminine in Fairy Tales*. Dallas: Spring Publications, 1980.

——. *Shadow and Evil in Fairy Tales*. Dallas: Spring Publications, 1983.

——. *Alchemy: An Introduction to the Symbolism and the Psychology*. Toronto: Inner City Press, 1982.

——. *On Divination and Synchronicity: The Psychology of Meaningful Chance*. Toronto: Inner City Press, 1981

Grattan-Guiness, I. (ed.) *Psychical Research: A Guide to its History, Principles and Practices. In Celebration of 100 Years of the Society for Psychic Research*. Wellingborough: 1982.

Greene, L. & H. Sasportas. *The Development of the Personality*. York Beach: Samuel Weiser, 1987.

Hagman, R. R. "A Study of Fears of Children of Preschool Age." From R. May: *The Meaning of Anxiety*. New York: Washington Square Press, 1979.

Hamaker-Zondag, K. M. *Handboek voor de uurhoekastrologie*. Amsterdam: Schors, 1983.

——. *Elements and Crosses as the Basis of the Horoscope*. York Beach: Samuel Weiser, 1984.

——. *Huisheren en huizenverbanden*. Amsterdam: Schors, 1984.

——. *Planetary Symbolism in the Horoscope*. York Beach: Samuel Weiser, 1985.

——. *Wat is toch astrologie?* Amsterdam: Schors, 1986.

——. *The Houses and Personality Development*. York Beach: Samuel Weiser, 1988.

——. *Aspects and Personality*. York Beach: Samuel Weiser, 1990.

——. *Psychological Astrology*. York Beach: Samuel Weiser, 1990.

Hannah, B. *Encounters with the Soul: Active Imagination as Developed by C. G. Jung*. Boston: Sigo Press, 1981.

Harding, M. E. *Psychic Energy: Its Source and Transformation*. Princeton University Press, 1973.

————. *The "I" and the "Not-I": A Study in the Development of Consciousness.* Princeton University Press, 1973.

Jacoby, J. *De psychologie van C. G. Jung. Een inleiding totzijn werk.* Zeist: 1963.

Jacoby, M. V., Kast en I. *Riedel: Das Bose im Marchen.* Fellbach: 1978.

Jaffe, A. *Geistererscheinungen und Vorzeichen.* Zurich: 1958.

Jersild, A. T. & F. B. Holmes. *Children's Fears.* New York: Teacher's College, Columbia University, 1935.

Jersild, A. T. *Child Psychology.* New York: 1940.

Johnson, R. A. *Inner Work: Using Dreams and Active Imagination for Personal Growth.* San Francisco: HarperCollins, 1986.

Jung, C.G. & R. Wilhelm. *Het geheim van de gouden bloem Een Chines levensboek.* Deventer, 1975.

Jung, C. G. *Memories, Dreams, Reflections.* New York: Pantheon, 1963.

————. *Analytical Psychology: Its Theory and Practice.* New York: Random House, 1970.

————. *Mandala Symbolism.* Princeton University Press, 1972.

————. *Synchronicity: A Causal Connecting Principle.* Princeton University Press, 1973.

————. *Het ik en het onbewuste.* Wassenaar: 1974.

————. *Collected Works*, Vol. 1–20. London: Routledge, 1978.

————. *Goed en kwaad in de westerse wereld.* Rotterdam: 1984.

Jung, E. *Animus and Anima.* Dallas: Spring Publications, 1985.

Kampherbeek, J. *800 Horoskopen van bekende menen.* Amsterdam: Schors, 1980.

Kankeleit, O. *Das Unbewusste als Keinstätte des Schöpferischen. Selbsterezeugnissen von Gelehrten, Dichtern und Künstlern.* Munich: 1958.

Kast, V. *Sprookjes als therapie.* Rotterdam: 1987.

Mattoon, M. A. *Understanding Dreams.* Dallas: Spring Publications, 1984.

May, R. *The Meaning of Anxiety.* New York: Washington Square Press, a division of Simon & Schuster, 1979.

Meier, C. A. *Die Empirie des Unbewussten.* Zurich: 1968.

Mindell, A. *Dreambody: The Body's Role in Revealing the Self.* London: 1984.

Moody, R. *The Light Beyond*. New York: Bantam, 1988.

Neumann, E. *The Origins and History of Consciousness*. Princeton University Press, 1970.

———. *The Great Mother: An Analysis of the Archetype*. Princeton University Press, 1974.

———. *The Child*. Boston: Shambhala, 1990.

Pearce, J. C. *Magical Child: Rediscovering Nature's Plan for our Children*. New York: Bantam, 1970.

Progoff, I. *Jung, Synchronicity and Human Destiny: Noncausal Dimensions of Human Experience*. New York: Crown, 1973.

Sanford, J. A. *The Invisible Partner*. Mahwah, NJ: Paulist Press, 1980.

Schwarz, B. E. *Psychic Nexus: Psychic Phenomena in Psychiatry and Everyday Life*. New York: Van Nos Reinhold, 1980.

Singer, J. L. *Dagdromen mag*. Haarlem, 1978. English: *The Inner World of Daydreaming*.

Spinelli, E. Paper read to the annual Convention of Parapsychological Assn. From: Ehrenwald J. *The ESP Experience*. 1976.

Stevenson, I. *Telepathic Impressions: A Review and Report of 35 New Cases*. Charlottesville: University of Virginia Press, 1970.

Tenhaeff, E. H. C. *Ontmoetingen met paragnosten*. Utrecht, z.j.

Verny, T. R. & J. Kelly. *The Secret Life of the Unborn Child*. New York: Dell, 1982.

Viorst, J. *Necessary Losses*. New York: Simon & Schuster, 1986.

Whitmont, E. C. *The Return of the Goddess: Feminity, Aggression and the Modern Grail Quest*. New York: Crossroad, 1984.

Wickes, F. G. *The Inner World of Choice*. London: Coventure, 1977.

———. *The Inner World of Childhood: A Study in Analytical Psychology*. Boston: Sigo Press, 1988.

Wilber, K. (ed.) *The Holographic Paradigm and other Paradoxes*.

Woodman, M. *Addiction to Perfection: The Still Unravished Bride*. Toronto: Inner City Press, 1982.

Karen Hamaker-Zondag is one of the leading members of the Astrological Foundation, *Arcturus*, in Holland. She is a graduate of the University of Amsterdam with doctoral degrees in social geography and environmental engineering. Her post-graduate study of psychology, astrology, and parapsychology has inspired a counseling practice where she combines Jungian concepts with astrological theory. She is the author of six other books also published by Weiser. She has lectured extensively in Holland, Belgium, Germany, England, the United States of America, Switzerland, Scandinavia, and Canada, and most recently lectured at the United Astrology Congress (UAC) in Washington, DC.